Reframing Decision Making
in Education

Reframing Decision Making in Education

Democratic Empowerment of Teachers and Parents

Perry R. Rettig

ROWMAN & LITTLEFIELD
Lanham • Boulder • New York • London

Published by Rowman & Littlefield
A wholly owned subsidiary of
The Rowman & Littlefield Publishing Group, Inc.
4501 Forbes Boulevard, Suite 200, Lanham, Maryland 20706
www.rowman.com

Unit A, Whitacre Mews, 26-34 Stannary Street, London SE11 4AB

Copyright © 2016 by Perry Rettig

All rights reserved. No part of this book may be reproduced in any form or by any electronic or mechanical means, including information storage and retrieval systems, without written permission from the publisher, except by a reviewer who may quote passages in a review.

British Library Cataloguing in Publication Information Available

Library of Congress Cataloging-in-Publication Data

Names: Rettig, Perry Richard, author.
Title: Reframing decision making in education : democratic empowerment of teachers and parents / Perry Rettig.
Description: Lanham, Maryland : Rowman & Littlefield, 2016. | Includes bibliographical references.
Identifiers: LCCN 2016009892 (print) | LCCN 2016021774 (ebook) | ISBN 9781475827187 (cloth : alk. paper) | ISBN 9781475827194 (pbk. : alk. paper) | ISBN 9781475827200 (Electronic)
Subjects: LCSH: School management and organization—United States—Decision making. | Teacher participation in administration—United States. | School management and organization—Parent participation—United States.
Classification: LCC LB2806 .R375 2016 (print) | LCC LB2806 (ebook) | DDC 371.2—dc23
LC record available at https://lccn.loc.gov/2016009892

∞™ The paper used in this publication meets the minimum requirements of American National Standard for Information Sciences—Permanence of Paper for Printed Library Materials, ANSI/NISO Z39.48-1992.

Printed in the United States of America

Reframing Decision Making in Education is dedicated to my wife and fellow professor, Dr. Jeri-Mae G. Astolfi. Her professional proclivity and career dedication continue to serve as an inspiration for me. She has served as my sounding board and confidant while pulling together these notions of empowering the broader education community. It is with this great appreciation that I dedicate this book to Jeri-Mae.

Contents

Preface	ix
Introduction	xvii
1 The Way Things Are	1
2 It Doesn't Have to Be This Way	27
3 Democratic Principles: Change Happens	63
4 Implications and Applications for Our Schools	99
5 Back to the Future	125
Bibliography	137
About the Author	145

Preface

Like most institutions, American public schools are governed using a model developed in a different era. Born of the Industrial Age, classical management systems have created very little substantive change as we have moved into this postmodern world. Our schools maintain a rigid hierarchy with a patriarchal, top-down emphasis. Administrators, school board members, teachers, and parents alike seem to be displeased with this status, yet no one seems to have an answer or to be willing to make the necessary dramatic changes.[1]

Some administrators may say this is an unfair characterization; they will indicate that they use participatory management practices, Site Councils, versions of quality circles, and shared decision making. However, it must be made clear, participation is not the same as democratic decision making. While the old classical rule of the iron fist may have been replaced by the gentler Human Relations approaches of "employee empowerment," administrators are still in control.

We have all heard supervisors say, "I want my people to feel empowered." But you can always tell an administrator's true colors when a committee makes a recommendation and then gets overturned by their boss. Professional educators, quite frankly, are frustrated by such manipulation.

In the immortal words of Eldridge Cleaver, "The heretical mailed fist of American reality rises to the surface in the velvet glove of our every institutionalized endeavor."[2] Perhaps Cleaver's words seem too inflammatory, too revolutionary. But the Human Relations management approaches common to so many schools today are actually quite manipulative. People are asked to participate, but their voices are seldom honestly recognized. In describing Aldous Huxley's *Brave New World*, Jermier illuminates this point:

> Social control in Huxley's world is more unobtrusive, beguiling, and seductive. Controllers neither torture nor kill. Citizens of the new world suffer no hardships, enjoy a high standard of living and, for the most part, find little cause to complain. Yet social control in Huxley's dystopia is just as comprehensive and programmed as it is in Orwell's. . . . Those who do resist are treated as if they are simply sick or maladjusted.[3]

I don't want teachers and parents to *feel* empowered; I want them to *be* empowered! It is my belief that there is a way to truly empower professional educators and even parents and students. In fact, the model has always been there for us. It is my sincere belief we should reexamine the fundamental principles upon which our democratic country was founded and apply them to school governance. Milton Derber wrote so eloquently that

> [p]eople may find it difficult to accept the use of democratic principles in organizations, but that was the original intention. During the American Revolution, Thomas Jefferson, James Madison, and other founding fathers envisioned the application of democracy to work life. Albert Gallatin, Secretary of the Treasury under Jefferson said, "The democratic principle on which this nation was founded should not be restricted to politics but should be applied to industry as well."[4]

Numerous authors have called for American institutions to establish democratic principles as the guiding values for organizational management—a form of workplace suffrage, if you will. Yet they indicate that these ideals are antithetical to our most cherished assumptions about how our systems are to be led.

For example, Gamson and Levin bemoaned, "It is a major anachronism of American society that democracy is defined as relevant only in the political sphere of life. The relative freedom of the political arena stands in sharp contrast to the authoritarian principles governing the American workplace."[5]

In a concurring opinion, Cheney et al. posited, "Within the context of organized labor, voice as a practical construct refers to autonomous practices of speech that are braced by institutional guarantees. The right of free speech guaranteed to U.S. citizens by the First Amendment largely disappears within the context of the workplace."[6]

Not only are our schools governed in an undemocratic and autocratic fashion, but our curriculum and pedagogy are, too. Teachers often have little legitimate authority in determining curriculum standards, content, materials, and assessment. Students clearly have the least say in their own education.[7]

It is thus imperative that "effective teachers reflect critically on the moral, political, social, and economic dimensions of education. This requires an understanding of multiple contexts in which schools function, an appreciation of diverse perspectives on educational issues, and a commitment to democratic forms of interaction."[8]

Again, it is my contention that our public school systems are governed in a way that is wholly inappropriate. I make this astonishing statement for three reasons. First, the classical model of organization and its management no longer fit in a postmodern age. Second, it seems only right to me that we model our schools in a congruent manner to the democratic principles we espouse.

Third, and most importantly, it is the right way to treat people. I have laid out a tough order. These are uncharted grounds, and we seem to have a most difficult time wrapping our minds around these concepts. Mimetic isomorphism, the idea that people lead their organizations by the only way they have ever seen, is perhaps one of the greatest obstacles to school reform.[9]

We need to create new ways of thinking about our school systems, the way they are organized, and the way they are governed. "It means discarding the Xerox machine that exists in each of our heads, and that seduces us into mistaking tired, generic formulas for fresh, distinct analysis," according to Linfield.[10] We have to move beyond the antiquated way of thinking that supervisors know more than the workers—between the thinkers and the doers—as this approach does not work in professional organizations.[11]

Where do we start this undertaking? Heckscher and Applegate give us a clue:

> We need to make at least two types of analyses. The first is why we need a new organizational model—what is wrong with bureaucracy, and has it really reached the end of its usefulness? The second is what the new form offers in the way of improvement. These are not simple tasks. Bureaucracy, for all its bad repute today, has been an enormously effective form of organization, greatly increasing human capacity to carry out large and complex projects. It will be displaced only by something significantly better.[12]

So we don't get rid of bureaucracy, hierarchy, and management. But we do take a serious look at their roles and their purposes. No part of the organization or position will be sacrosanct in this discussion. But, again, we don't have to reinvent the wheel. The model has always been with us.

"Management could be far more effective if we drew on the power of our American heritage: democracy and enterprise. . . . The unpleasant truth is that we have relegated our principles to lofty occasions, such as presidential elections, while ignoring their relevance to our workplaces, schools, hospitals, churches, and other ordinary aspects of our daily life."[13]

In the very prescient words of Apple and Beane, "To say that democracy rests on the consent of the governed is almost cliché, but in a democratic school it is true that all of those directly involved in the school, including the young people, have the right to participate in the process of decision making."[14]

I do wish to make one significant note here. Throughout this book, the reader will note that I use the term "bureaucracy." It is not my intent to use this in a derogatory manner as is so common in today's vernacular. Rather, I use the term to designate middle and lower management positions with specialized training and functions within the school district. It is not meant to denote people who are uncaring automatons but a recognition of their work and responsibilities.

As will become apparent in the latter chapters of this book, I am framing a governance model fairly well aligned with that of the U.S.

federal government. Other models, such as unicameral or parliamentary, could be used. However, I am not in favor of a model of one-person, one-vote. Rather, I am in favor of a representational model, certainly in the early Tier stages. This is the model presented in this book.

My purpose in writing this book is atypical in that I don't look at school reform to provide ways in which to make schools more effective or efficient. Such reform initiatives have already been tried. "It should come as no surprise that most formal attempts at democratizing work have tended to place the goal of productivity well above the social goal of valuing democracy for its own sake or for the benefits it can give to society."[15]

Rather, I have written this book with altruistic motives. I wish to challenge our notions about how to govern our schools so that we treat people with dignity and respect, because that is the right thing to do. And I believe that our founding democratic principles are the best place to start.

We espouse democratic principles, but are our actions within our organizations congruent? I know that they are not, and it is my goal to help us consider how to realign our thinking, our governance, and our structures to make this so. This task is being made all the more difficult as the federal and state governments are taking power away from local school districts by stipulating curricular standards and onerous assessment protocols.

I believe you will finish this book with more questions than answers; but that's as it should be. After all, the answers should come from a collective democratic dialogue with you and those who make up your school community. Please allow the following chapters to ignite this dialogue. American democracy began with a revolution, and it may take just such a local revolution to reclaim our schools. In the words of Paulo Freire, the famous author of *Pedagogy of the Oppressed*, "Radicalization, nourished by a critical spirit, is always creative."[16]

NOTES

1. Nohria and Berkley succinctly captured the disconnect between today's managers working in yesterday's organizations:

In [Daniel] Bell's view, the cohesive worldview of the American 1950s—exemplified in the nearly iconic status of factories and large industrial organizations—had all but disappeared, leaving a social void in a world in which these older icons were increasingly seen as anachronisms.

Nitin Nohria and James D. Berkley, "The Virtual Organization: Bureaucracy, Technology, and the Implosion of Control," in Charles Heckscher and Lynda Applegate, eds., *The Post-Bureaucratic Organization: New Perspectives on Organizational Change* (Thousand Oaks, CA: Sage, 1994), 109.

2. Eldridge Cleaver, *Soul on Ice* (New York: Dell Publishing, 1968), 84.

3. J. Jermier, "Critical Perspectives on Organizational Control," *Administrative Science Quarterly* 4 (1998): 245.

4. Milton Derber, *The American Idea of Democracy* (Chicago: University of Chicago Press, 1970), 6. John Dewey added, "The movement for the democratic idea inevitably became a movement for publicly conducted and administered schools," in John Dewey, *Democracy and Education* (Carbondale, IL: Southern Illinois University, 2008), 99.

5. Zelda F. Gamson and Henry M. Levin, "Obstacles to the Survival of Democratic Workplaces," in Robert Jackall and Henry M. Levin, eds., *Worker Cooperatives in America* (Berkeley, CA: University of California Press, 1984), 219.

6. George Cheney et al., "Democracy, Participation, and Communication at Work: A Multidisciplinary Review," in *Communication Yearbook* 21 (2004): 64.

7. Gamson and Levin further elucidated:

> Schools tend to be impersonal, bureaucratic, and hierarchical, like the typical workplace. Course grades and promotion in the school are similar to wages and salaries and job advancement in the workplace. Expulsion or academic failure have their counterparts in job loss and unemployment. In both the workplace and the school, the activity of the student (workers) is determined by factors external to them, such as the curriculum (production activity), the organization of instruction (production), and the instructional materials (tools) that will be used. Supervision and evaluation are carried out by teachers (work supervisors) whose authority derives solely from their superior positions in the organizational hierarchy. These supervisors control the content of the work activity as well as the rewards and sanctions, and successful students learn quickly to accept the norms of the organization.

Zelda F. Gamson and Henry M. Levin, "Obstacles to the Survival of Democratic Workplaces," in Robert Jackall and Henry M. Levin, eds., *Worker Cooperatives in America* (Berkeley, CA: University of California Press, 1984), 224.

8. K. Sirotnik, "What You See Is What You Get: Consistency, Persistency, and Mediocrity in Classrooms," *Harvard Educational Review* 53 (1983): 16.

9. For a more detailed description of mimetic isomorphism, see Mark S. Mizruchi and Lisa C. Fein, "The Social Construction of Organizational Knowledge: A Study of the Uses of Coercive, Mimetic, and Normative Isomorphism," *Administrative Science Quarterly* 44(4) (December 1999): 679.

10. Susie Linfield, "The Treason of the Intellectuals (Again)," in George Packer, ed., *The Fight Is for Democracy* (New York: Harper Collins, 2003), 181.

11. Teresa M. Harrison, "Designing the Post-Bureaucratic Organization: New Perspectives on Organizational Change," in *Australian Journal of Communication* 19 (Brisbane, Australia, 1992): 21, "Success . . . thus requires a form of work organization that eradicates the distinction between those who plan work and those who execute it."

12. Charles Heckscher and Lynda Applegate, "Introduction," in Charles Heckscher and Anne Donnellon, eds., *The Post-Bureaucratic Organization: New Perspectives on Organizational Change* (Thousand Oaks, CA: Sage, 1994): 4.

13. William E. Halal, *The New Management: Bringing Democracy and Markets Inside Organizations* (San Francisco: Berrett-Koehler, 1998), 255.

14. Michael W. Apple and James A. Beane, eds., *Democratic Schools, Second Edition: Lessons in Powerful Education* (London, UK: Heinemann Publishing, 2007), 10.

15. B. Schiller, "Workplace Democracy: The Dual Roots of Worker Participation," in D. Hancock, J. Logue, and B. Schiller, eds., *Managing Modern Capitalism: Industrial Renewal and Workplace Democracy in the United States and Western Europe* (New York: Praeger, 1991) 109–20.

16. Paulo Freire, *Pedagogy of the Oppressed* (New York: Continuum, 1970), 37.

Introduction

This book will begin with a brief description of our current education organizational enterprise, how it got this way, and why the model is inappropriate. We will do this examination through the lens of Critical Theory. From this foundation, we will then investigate emerging, contemporary organic theories in organizational administration and discuss how they can be applied to the creation of a cogent new model of educational leadership and the governance of schools.[1]

Chapter 3 reserves a special essay written by a current board of education member from rural Ohio. This essay shares a local school district's turbulent journey from organizational dysfunction to a model resembling shared governance.

This chapter will be followed by a thorough examination of the democratic principles that are of particular importance to the governance of public schools. This book will conclude with an analysis of how these principles could be applied. Because schools are embedded in a variety of contexts with all kinds of constituents, this analysis will be divided into three parts.

Tier I will focus on the most fundamental democratic principles that all schools should utilize. Tier II will provide a description of how these principles could be implemented more extensively beyond professional staff governance into the areas of parental involvement and district-wide systemic governance issues.

Tier III might appear more utopian, or it might be more useful for starting a democratically centered charter school or individual private school. Woven throughout this book, you will find a narrative of a fictitious principal. You will see how "Sam" struggles and moves her middle school from its traditional governance and management base to a more democratic model.

Each chapter concludes with a listing of Key Points and a section of Points to Ponder. These points could serve as a good reflection device for local site groups to gather and enter into a meaningful dialogue as they consider grappling with the notion of democratic governance.

NOTE

1. In no way can these early sections be considered an authoritative analysis of their subjects. For much more descriptive study of these topics, the reader is invited to read the books and articles noted at the end of each chapter and as outlined in the annotated bibliography. However, the model that will be presented later in this book is more systemically structured and comprehensive than might be found in isolated schools, such as the Sudbury Schools that can be found across the country, or the European Democratic Education Community. For more information about these democratic school approaches, the reader is encouraged to visit the websites www.sudburyschool.com and www.eudec.org.

CHAPTER 1

The Way Things Are

The management and organizational structure of American public schools has seen very little substantive change since the Industrial Age. When our country was primarily an agrarian nation, schools were much smaller and locally run. Teachers had less professional expertise, but they also had more autonomy.

The Scientific Revolution and the Industrial Age, on the other hand, had tremendous implications for the management of not only the nation's manufacturing sector but for the management of public schools, as well. Over time, schools got bigger, teachers received more technical training, but they lost much of their autonomy and power. The era of bureaucracy was born, and very little has truly changed in the organization and administration of our schools.

How did this happen? A confluence of two major events brought these changes about. First, the classical Newtonian sciences gained preeminence. Second, the Industrial Age became dominant. Together, they created the science of organizational administration.

Sir Isaac Newton is considered the father of the classical sciences. Classical physics begins with the premise that objectivity leads to predictability. In order to make predictions, the researcher must be completely objective; there must be a separation of the subject and the object. Robert Palter explained the Newtonian "hypothetico-deductive method" as encompassing three critical parts: formulation, deduction, and testing.[1]

The researcher needs to control the experiment, manipulate the variables, and observe the changes. Each variable (in theory) can be quantified through this process; every conceivable variable can be given a numerical value and placed into a formula. By isolating the variables, the researcher can then replicate the experiment, seek consistency, and ultimately predictability and control.

It's quite apparent that classical physics is founded on linear, mechanistic thinking. The foundation of this science is a study of the parts in a reductionistic way of looking at *things*. The notion of *things* is so very important to classical physics. This physics has the aim of reducing the whole into ever smaller parts.

The idea is that if we can break the whole into small enough parts, we can study those parts individually, and then put them back together to better understand the whole. This is relatively easy with closed systems such as machines. Each component is taken apart, studied in detail, and put back together. For the purposes here, the key principles of classical sciences are:[2]

- Reductionism
- Objectivity
- Control
- Replication
- Prediction

The classical sciences provided the framework for the scientific study of organizations; Frederick Taylor provided the scholarship.

An American with an engineering background, Taylor believed that organizations could be studied and rationally understood. His time and motion studies were conducted in order to organize each type of work so that time and effort were minimized. Basic features of this model are well known to all who have studied leadership. In order to provide for routine performance, there must be a standardization of tasks. Through a division of labor there is a specialization of tasks. While there is a *specialization* of tasks, they become *standardized* within their specialization.

An impersonal hierarchy is necessary and is established through a pyramid model where the optimal number of people under any one person's span of control should be five to ten workers. This impersonal orientation is designed to treat all people alike and to keep decisions objective and rational. There must also be a uniqueness of function where each department does its own work, and there should not be any duplication of work by other departments.

Finally, the formal connections within the organization are indicated on an organizational blueprint or flowchart of hierarchy and job responsibilities. This scientific movement to the understanding of organizations had profound effects on the structuring and management of these systems. Taylor conceptualized four principles of scientific management:

1. Eliminate the guesswork of rule-of-thumb approaches to deciding how each worker is to do a job by adopting scientific measurements to break the job down into a series of small, related tasks.
2. Use more scientific, systematic methods for selecting workers and training them for specific jobs.
3. Establish a clear division of responsibility between management and workers, with management doing the goal setting, planning, and supervising and workers executing the required tasks.
4. Establish the discipline whereby management sets the objectives and the workers cooperate in achieving them.[3]

These principles of scientific management played a central role in the design of administration in this new era.

Large organizations were the by-product of the Industrial Age. The industrial leaders needed ways to understand and manage these monolithic structures. The machines that were created in these factories served as a model for the organization of their own industries. Closed Systems thinking was born, and the machine metaphor served as its exemplar. Industrialists thought that they could run their manufacturing systems like the machines they made, and in fact, they did manage their organizations in a corresponding fashion.

Closed Systems thinking is all about efficiency and effectiveness. The goal is to maximize productivity. It is a positivistic or deterministic approach that requires linear, rational decision making. The Newtonian sciences led to Closed Systems thinking and provided the theoretical framework for the development of an industrial model for organizational structure and governance.

French industrialist Henri Fayol had executive-level work experience, and he began the actual study of Classical Organizational Thought. "He advocated that all managers perform five basic functions: planning, organizing, commanding, coordinating, and controlling."[4] Still, Fayol advocated that administrators use these principles flexibly and that they use judgment in carrying out their responsibilities.

This lesson seems to have been overlooked by many of our contemporary administrators. According to notable systems thinker Peter Block, "We govern our organizations by valuing, above all else, consistency, control, and predictability."[5]

Max Weber—a German sociologist—concerned about arbitrary power in the hands of the few, formulated bureaucratic structures in order to legitimize authority in the hands of experts.[6] Structurally, Weber believed that all good organizations should share certain characteristics for the purpose of efficiency. First, they all should have a division of labor and specialization. For example, there are various levels and departments, and each unit and position has specific responsibilities.

Second, there should be an impersonal orientation. This allows administrators to make decisions based upon facts, not feelings, and to treat each person equally. Third, all organizations needs a hierarchy of authority. This provides for clear patterns of communication and guarantees that workers will carry out their superiors' orders. Fourth, good systems need rules and regulations understood by all employees. This stipulation ensures uniformity and stability of employee work.

Finally, bureaucratic organizations require a career orientation. With this guarantee, quality work is rewarded with promotion. While Weber promoted bureaucratic structures, he was also concerned that bureaucracies could become too strong, and therefore, dangerous. This seems to be yet another lesson lost on many of our contemporary leaders. But as organizations get bigger, the more the differentiation, academic specialization, and bureaucratization.[7]

Critics of the Weberian Model have always existed. They point out that such bureaucratization hurts staff morale and causes worker boredom. These same critics claim that communication patterns are not more efficient,[8] that workers have no control of their goals and work environment, and that there is a conflict between achievement and seniority. Charles Heckscher argued, "All of Weber's forms of legitimate authority are essentially structures of domination—that is, contexts in which the higher level can command *without giving a justification* [italics in original]."[9]

Bureaucratic practices also produce legalism—where frustrated workers follow their job descriptions to the letter, not working to their full potential. Feminists feel that these organizations are gender-biased. And, most interestingly, the Weberian Model assumes that subordinates have less technical expertise than their superiors.[10] This last point is critical to our understanding of today's school culture. The hidden assumption is that teachers and professional staff know less than the administrators.

Mihaly Csikszentmihalyi warned, "The evidence suggests that the Industrial Revolution not only shortened the life spans of members of several generations, but made them more nasty and brutish as well."[11] Again, Max Weber created bureaucratic structures in order to make organizations more efficient, the work of the workers less ambiguous, and to take the power out of the hands of the few.

But according to Francis X. Neumann Jr., "The Weberian bureaucracy was totally suitable to a Weberian world, for a world of industrial or second wave society, but it may not be altogether appropriate for the new and more complex environments [of today]."[12]

These concerns have led practitioners and scholars alike to consider that classical organizations are, in fact, not very efficient. They began to believe that in order to make workers more efficient, they needed to make the work environment more collegial. In other words, "a happy worker is a productive worker." This led to the birth of a new model—the Human Relations Approach.

HUMAN RELATIONS IDEOLOGY

Like all Closed Systems theories, the Human Relations Approach still had the primary focus of efficiency in organizations. This approach is also considered Closed Systems thinking because management still controls and manipulates the system, albeit in a friendlier, gentler manner. Mary Parker Follett was not a strict adherent to Classical Organizational Thought.

As a sociologist, she saw the importance of administrators working with their workers as opposed to dictating to them. Likewise, she believed that decisions should be contingent upon the context of the situation—a precursor to contingency theory. Her research led her to postulate four principles of administration:

1. coordination by direct contact of the responsible people concerned,
2. coordination in the early stages,
3. coordination as the reciprocal relating of all the factors in the situation, and
4. coordination as a continuing process.

Parker advocated that decisions be made by those closest to where the decisions would be impacted. And both vertical and horizontal communication paths need to be utilized across and up through the organization. The third principle requires departments and units to be able to coordinate, in a flexible manner, their efforts in order to meet the organization's demands. The fourth principle "recognizes that management is an ever-changing, dynamic process in response to emerging situations—a sharp contrast to traditional, static, classical views that sought to codify universal principles of action."[13]

The now famous Hawthorne Studies helped shape the Human Relations movement. From these experiments, the social side of work dynamics proved to be certainly as important as the technical side. According to Owens:

> New concepts were now available to the administrator to use in practice. Among them were (1) morale, (2) group dynamics, (3) democratic supervision, (4) personnel relations, and (5) behavioral concepts of motivation. The human relations movement emphasized human and interpersonal factors in administering the affairs of organizations. Supervisors, in particular, drew heavily on human relations concepts, stressing such notions as "democratic" procedures, "involvement," motivational techniques, and the sociometry of leadership.[14]

Thus, a new generation of organizational researchers began emphasizing interpersonal aspects of the workplace with a focus on participation, cooperation, and collaboration. The role of administrators required dramatic changes. Russ Marion caught the essence of these new management strategies:

> Human Relations theorists approached leadership in terms of facilitating cooperative behavior, providing opportunity for personal growth, and dealing with human needs. Administrators were advised to communicate openly with workers, counsel those with personal problems, create a friendly comfortable work environment, be attentive to the human side of workers, project positive expectations about worker behavior, and deal effectively with informal groups.[15]

Therefore, the Human Relations movement put a more human face on the way administrators interacted with their workers. But make no doubt about it, the Human Relations Approach was still a Closed Systems model with the primary purpose of worker efficiency. In other words, managers treated their workers more humanely, gave them a larger role in decision making, and created a climate of collegiality for the primary purpose of making them work better.

Critics say that management's concern for workers is inauthentic in the Human Relations Approach. Rather, they say, these gentler and kinder practices are subtle ways for management to manipulate employees. It is as if the superiors are saying to their subordinates, "We'll make you happy as long as your work is excellent."

Other critics of Human Relations models are concerned about the lack of accountability and inconsequential supervisory strategies. They feel that the pendulum had shifted too far from autocratic authoritarianism to laissez-faire relativism. Organizations need structures, and employees need accountability and supervision.

VESTIGES OF THE IDEOLOGIES IN OUR SCHOOLS

Criticisms of the Scientific Management Approach, the Human Relations Approach, and bureaucracies abound. "Eventually, the self-defeating effects of naked authoritarianism became evident in sagging morale, skyrocketing turnover, worker sabotage, costly strikes, and low-quality products."[16] Cheney and Brancato lamented that "despite the fact that scientific management had appropriated some of the rhetorical power of the Progressive Movement, it jettisoned the Progressives' vision of a more participative, more democratic workplace."[17]

Scientist and postmodern systems thinker Margaret Wheatley exclaimed, "A mechanical world feels distinctly anti-human."[18] Finally, professor of management at George Washington University William Halal bemoaned, "The hierarchical model . . . continued to dominate the Industrial Age because it was good at managing routine tasks performed by *uneducated* [italics added] workers . . . but the former management system in which decisions flowed from the top down is now history."[19] Yet our public schools, like most organizations, are so very thoroughly entrenched in Closed Systems thinking.

Douglas McGregor was famous for conceptualizing two fundamentally discrete ways administrators can view, and subsequently supervise, their employees. These opposing views are known as Theory X and Theory Y. Closed Systems thinking understands human motivation through a Theory X perspective. The basic features of Theory X are:

- Average people are by nature indolent—they work as little as possible.
- They lack ambition, dislike responsibility, prefer to be led.
- They are inherently self-centered, indifferent to organizational needs.
- They are by nature resistant to change.
- They are gullible, not very bright, ready dupes of the charlatan and demagogue.[20]

From his own research Edward Greenberg stipulated, "In such a hierarchical system of supervision, workers are treated not as autonomous, rational, and responsible people but as persons to be watched, carefully managed, and compelled to work. Workers frequently mentioned that they were treated . . . as children."[21]

This certainly is not a very pleasant view of workers in our organizations. But a majority of practicing school administrators may well subconsciously have this picture in mind. Certainly they can think of staff members who work as little as possible, are lazy, indolent, dislike responsibility, are indifferent to the needs of the organization, and resistant to change. Even if principals don't have a Theory X view of most of their professional staff members, the supervisory practices and school policies they use support Theory X thinking—as we will discover later in this chapter.

For the sake of this discussion, there might be considered three salient themes that have emerged from the scholarship on Classical Organizational Thought.

1. A need for *bureaucratic hierarchy*: This allows all members of the organization a clear understanding of communication patterns and legitimized lines of authority. It also demarcates a span of control for supervision and decision making.
2. A *specialization of functions*: Specialized, scientific training provides for better efficiencies and more effectiveness in work. Management plans, organizes, commands, coordinates, and controls—they do the thinking. Employees carry out the work prescribed by management.
3. An *impersonal orientation*: Rules and regulations, carried out via cold and sterile precision, allow all workers to be treated equitably. Decisions are made objectively and without cronyism.

The Human Relations Approach brought with it two major changes to organizational management:

1. The need for a *friendly and healthy work environment*: In order for people to work better, morale needed to be maintained, opportunities for personal growth were considered important, and personal counseling for employees needed to be available.
2. The importance of the *informal group*: Group dynamics now took on a major focus. Employees were asked to work cooperatively with their peers, to collaborate collegially, to participate in decision making, and to communicate openly.

Let us now turn our attention to how these key attributes of Closed Systems thinking have manifested themselves in our contemporary school organizations.

The traditional or classical models of administration expect a great deal of control and authority by those in leadership positions.[22] "In this largely quantitative world, scientific management seems to make sense—command and control, management-by-objective, solving problems by reductionist analysis of its parts, etc."[23]

Archon Fung was discouraged in his analysis of most contemporary school governance systems. "In hierarchical models, accountability runs top-down, with central supervisors specifying methods and ends, and monitoring subordinates to see that they comply."[24] Hence the saying, when *you* expect, *you* must inspect.

In *Deepening Democracy*, Fung and coauthor Erik Wright stipulated that common practices of employee participation are less than truly empowering (akin to Human Relations Approaches): "Empowered participatory decision-making can be contrasted with three more familiar methods of social choice: *command and control* by experts, *aggregative voting,* and *strategic negotiation* [all italics in original]."[25]

John Smyth of Flinders University of South Australia made a clear distinction between modern approaches to organizational management and what a postmodern ideology could mean to our schools:

> The metaphor that comes from the prevailing view of leadership and administration as applied unquestionably to schools, is highly derivative of a largely abandoned and outmoded Newtonian view of mechanics, the military, and business. It is about missioning, controlling, commanding, operational and strategic planning, and surveillance. If we were to depart from this militaristic metaphor, there is a distinct chance several things might happen, according to Sergiovanni (1994):
>
> - there would be much less preoccupation with who is in control;
> - there would be less emphasis on contractual relationships;
> - there would be much less equating of hierarchy with expertise.[26]

The classrooms have been especially affected by the classical sciences approaches. In 1999, the National Research Council wrote:

> School administrators [are] eager to make use of the "scientific" organization of factories to structure efficient classrooms. Children [are] regarded as raw materials to be efficiently processed by technical work-

ers (the teachers) to reach the end product. . . . Teachers [are] viewed as workers whose job [is] to carry out directives from their superiors—the efficiency experts of schooling (administrators and researchers).[27]

If you were to ask most principals whether they practiced autocratic leadership, they would probably be offended. The majority of school administrators would find that themselves falling into one of two categories. Some would consider themselves firm, yet fair. They are paid to make the tough decisions and provide vision for their schools. Their teachers look to them for direction and a sense of security.

The second group includes "people" persons. Their style of leadership is that of colleague and "guide on the side." They help build a culture of family and community that inspires people to strive for optimal effectiveness. Administrators in both groups are most likely to practice situational leadership by altering their behavior depending on the circumstances.

After all, this is not a one-size-fits-all world. Still, even in this era of site-based management, peer supervision, and professional associations, most administrators (both building-level and central office) primarily show tendencies of Classical Scientific Management or the Human Relations Approach, or a mixture of both.

Our school systems are as rigidly structured as they were when they first adopted their industrial strictures. The hierarchy remains a top-down governance and communication model wherein different silos (departments and subject areas) are aligned for efficiency and standardization. District administrators sit atop these management pyramids.

In most districts, reporting directly to these district CEOs are a series of deputies, or directors, or assistant superintendents. Each of these middle managers has specialized functions and responsibilities. For instance, there quite likely is a director of human resources, a director of business services, a director of pupil services, and a director of curriculum and instruction. With the exception of the Personnel Department, each of these directors will supervise five to ten people with additional expertise.

The director of pupil services may well supervise professional staff with specialization in learning disabilities, emotional and behavioral disabilities, cognitive disabilities, and physical disabilities. School social workers and psychologists might also report to this director. In cases where several bureaucrats work within a specialized area, coordinators might be assigned to them. For example, a district that employees a half a dozen or more school psychologists and social workers could very well have coordinators for both of these specialties.

The director of business services will directly supervise a controller (interesting title for a manager), an MIS manager, a coordinator of purchasing and shipping, a coordinator of food services, and a coordinator of buildings and grounds. Again, each of these coordinators likely has other bureaucrats working under their command.

The director of curriculum and instruction will most likely have coordinators in the areas of reading and language arts, foreign languages, mathematics, science, social sciences, ESL/bilingual, art, music, physical education and health, gifted and talented, and perhaps testing and assessment. Often there are coordinators who wear multiple hats.

Each of these major function areas (human resources, business services, pupil services, and curriculum and instruction) has its own systems of accountability and bureaucracy. Tedious and microscopic budgeting processes provide answerability for business services, while personnel services use very prescriptive collective bargaining agreements.

Pupil services is clearly governed by federal and state laws that detail how students, teachers, and programs are identified, serviced, and evaluated. Curriculum and instruction has numerous committees that must proceed through various levels of acquiescence for curricular changes and textbook adoption. Student and curricula assessments are the hallmark of accountability in this function area.

The entire organization is governed by literally hundreds of impersonal policies that are developed and approved by the administration and the board of education. Communication is clearly funneled through pyramidal flow charts. E-mail and memoranda rule the day. Command, control, replication—this static blueprint is found invariably throughout our country.

School district budgets are most often highly centralized. State-standardized accounting systems are mandated. Clearly, the process is extremely structured. The largest expenditure of each district budget—staff salaries and benefits—is under the auspices of the central office bureaucrats. The next largest set of district expenditures, facilities management and technology, is typically under the control of the centralized office of business services.

On the other hand, schools are allocated, by central office management, a nominal per-pupil amount. At the building level, principals often decide how much money is allotted to each teacher, unit, or department. With this money teachers are expected to buy supplies and supplemental materials for their instruction. Ultimately, very little money (outside of salaries and benefits) is directly provided to the teachers—those people who work most closely with the students.

The budgeting process demands consistency, control, and standardization. While good arguments can be made that school system budgeting is an area that can and should be standardized and controlled, the point here is not to change contemporary accounting procedures. Rather, the point is that more autonomy should be given to the local level for budgeting decisions.

Even individual school sites are structured systems within the larger system. There is a principal at the top of the hierarchy with various assistants and department chairs reporting to him or her. Both administrators and teachers alike follow the same policies and procedures as the central bureaucrats.

The superintendent is responsible for providing supervision and evaluation of the directors, who in turn are responsible for the supervision and evaluation of their coordinators. Either the district administrator or assistants are also responsible for providing supervision and evaluation of building principals. Likewise, the principals are then expected to provide clinical supervision and evaluation of teachers, as well as classified staff—right down the hierarchy.

Sadly, teachers often complain that the supervision that they receive is more perfunctory in practice and meaningless to them, and their summative evaluations are not based upon a holistic view.[28] Professional faculty are observed very infrequently and then receive a written report as to the effectiveness of their teaching. The summative evaluations at the end of the year are typically based upon these infrequent observation reports.

These observation and evaluation forms are very prescriptive and detailed in what is expected of the teachers and in the levels of their performance. Each teacher is rated using the same forms. Individualized supervision and evaluation are the exception, not the rule. Forms are the standard, and personal development plans are cursory, at best. It's as if quality teaching can be captured on a checklist and replicated to all settings—one size fits all. Consistency, control, and standardization are valued as desirable.

The National Research Council stipulated, "The factory model affect[s] the design of the curriculum, instruction, and assessment in schools.[29] Teachers typically are not permitted to unilaterally choose their own textbooks and curriculum. They generally must follow the prescribed curriculum guides provided by the school district. Likewise, teachers must use textbooks that have been written by external publishers and adopted by the board of education.

There is renewed interest in state and national curricula. There is an emphasis on consistency and standardization. Many of these textbooks attempt to "teacher proof" the job of educators. Furthermore, there is an increasing emphasis at both the state and federal levels for standardization of assessment and testing of students. In other words, the curriculum, the instruction, and the assessment tools are becoming more and more homogeneous and similar from school to school.

There is an increasing desire to make each school look alike. The No Child Left Behind Act has made sure of this. In a chilling review of the path American education has followed, education expert Linda Darling-Hammond warned:

> Our inheritance from the assembly line is the notion that decision making about curriculum, assessments, school design, and student progress is the purview of those who sit above teachers in a large bureaucracy. Teachers' work consists largely of stamping students with lessons as they pass by, conveyer belt style, from grade to grade and class period to class period.[30]

Current decision-making practices are clearly impacted by Closed Systems thinking. Whether Classical Scientific Management or Human Relations orientation, these prototypical models share one thing in common when it comes to decision making—both ultimate authority and ultimate responsibility rest in the office of the administration.

Organizations that use a Classical Scientific Management approach to management processes view decision making as something explicitly under the purview of the supervisor or boss. Everyone in the organization knows who makes the decisions. It is the proverbial iron fist approach. These kinds of administrators might be heard saying something like, "I do the hiring, and I do the firing." On the other hand, employees might reply by saying, "At least you know where the boss stands." The classical model is based on unilateral, linear decision-making processes—clear, clean, and precise.

Administrators are taught how to make rational decisions. They learn to define the problem, analyze it considering all the variables, identify possible solutions considering a multitude of factors including who is impacted, and then choose the best solution. Vroom and Yetton created a normative leadership flow chart to depict this rational, linear decision-making process (see figure 1.1).[31] Organizational scientists have defined seven steps to any rational decision-making process:

1. Define the decision,
2. identify the alternatives,
3. assess the alternatives,
4. select the best possible alternative,
5. secure acceptance of the decision,
6. implement the decision, and
7. evaluate the decision.[32]

In order to maximize worker efficiency, the Human Relations Approach to management saw the need to consider employees' emotional engagement and needs. In these types of organizations, workers can hear their supervisors saying such things as, "I want my employees to *feel* empowered." More constituents are brought in to sit on committees. Often they are taught how to make rational decisions, again by considering all the factors, analyzing potentials, and making the best choice. They then make their recommendation to the administration for final authority.

If the administration and the *empowered* committee members disagree, the administration plays their trump card. Ultimately, the process is still the same—very linear and rationalistic with administration

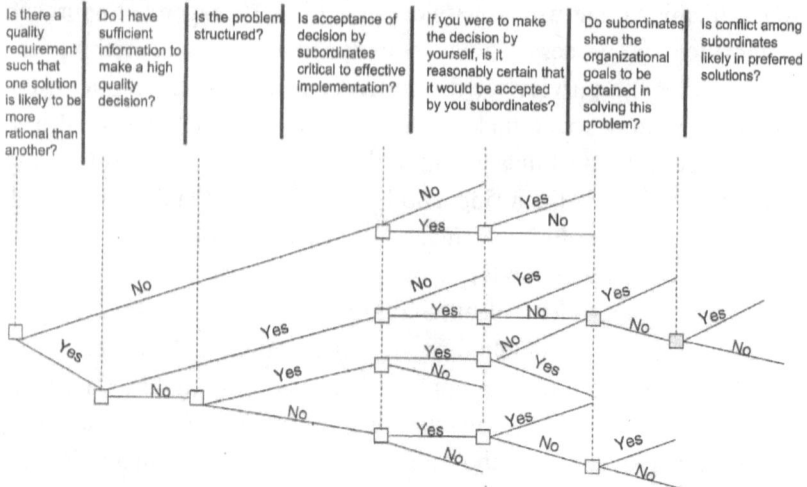

Figure 1.1. *Vroom-Yelton decision making flow chart*

as the ultimate authority. It's the proverbial iron fist wrapped in a velvet glove. Workers feel that at least with the old model they knew they had little say. The more modern approach leads workers on to *feel* they are empowered. When they find out that they are not really empowered, they become disenfranchised and morale begins to slip.

Teaching staff are not the only ones alienated in the prototypical school organizational model. Students are at the bottom of the heap, and their level of influence is commensurate. Noam Chomsky bemoaned:

> Schools [are] institutions for indoctrination and for imposing obedience. Far from creating independent thinkers, schools have always, throughout history, played an institutional role in a system of control and coercion. And once you are well educated, you have already been socialized in ways that support the power structure, which in turn rewards you immensely.[33]

The vestiges of Classical Organizational Thought and the Human Relations Approach are so thoroughly engrained in our organizational psyche that we don't even question their impact on our work lives. We simply take their presumptions for granted, and "the way things are"—

our mimetic isomorphism. The remainder of this book will examine these presumptions and not accept things "the way they are."

SAM I AM

Sitting on the north bend of the Chegwalia River, Washington High School overlooks this hardworking city. Washington High is supported by four middle schools and ten elementary schools. It has a population of 1,530 students, 26 paraprofessionals, and nearly 80 faculty. They are led by Samantha Levy, who is in her second year as principal. She is supported by her young athletic director, Billy Westbrook, and by her associate principal, Evan Moore.

This community cannot be categorized as primarily either working-class, industrial or white collar, upper middle class. It really is quite eclectic in its demographics, and the high school is a microcosm of the city it represents. While New LaCerne has its roots in heavy industry, much has changed over the last two decades or so. New LaCerne has embraced the IT industry, and its demographics have begun to reflect this shift.

Sam Levy always knew she would be a principal. But it happened to her quicker than she thought. She taught American history and served as assistant principal in the Midwest for six years while working on her master's degree in educational administration. She moved to New LaCerne to be a middle school principal, which lasted for one year. She was seen as a star on the rise and was selected last year as the principal of Washington High School. Her first year as a head principal was a blur, as she was in "survival mode" on a day-to-day basis. She came into the second year ready to show her leadership, even though she didn't quite know her leadership style or tendencies. But this would prove to be a pivotal year for Samantha.

Throughout her first year as a high school principal, Sam felt uneasy in being considered a superior to other professionals and in the way that her administrative colleagues were cavalier in their attitude about their authority. She was disarmed when the director of Human Resources questioned her about her decisiveness. Sam told Lawrence Vogel that she and her Site Council representatives were having difficulty in deciding whom to hire for a new physical education teacher position. The teachers wanted one candidate, while she preferred another one. Lawrence asked her emphatically, "Who's the boss at Washington?" Sam stammered that she was and made the decision to hire her favorite candidate.

Then there was the time last winter when a special administrator meeting was called for all principals and the directors of the central offices. The topic was extremely confidential and was not to be discussed beyond the walls of the conference room. Due to reductions in state aid, declining enrollments, and additional unfunded mandates—the trifecta of fiscal nightmares—the district was required to cut nearly $2 million out of the next budget. Superintendent Carleson charged the administrative leadership with producing two optional plans to meet these cuts. One plan included extracurricular cuts, and the other plan left these programs alone. These deliberations were to remain secret, according to Michael Carleson, because he didn't want to start a panic or "turf wars" among the various staffs and departmental units.

There were so many other examples of authoritative arrogance that Samantha questioned whether she had what it takes to be an administrator. She had noted for years that there was an aura of superiority in administrators, "the suits," as dispassionately called by the teachers. Sam found herself wearing, in fact, more businesslike attire last year. In order to seem less detached from her faculty, she decided to dress a little less formally this year.

The political election season brought all these concerns to mind as Samantha sat in her office planning the agenda for tomorrow's Washington Site Council meeting. Samantha didn't recall any special training in putting together meeting agendas; she simply followed the agenda format from previous principals at Washington—she hadn't made any changes to it. Scanning down the draft, Sam was uninspired.

Washington High School
Site Council Agenda
September 12

1. Approval of Minutes from June 1
2. Old Business
    a. Washington goals
    b. Supervision schedule

  c. Budget allocations
  d. Student assessment
 3. New Business
  a. Teacher assessment
  b. Curriculum initiatives
 4. Other Business
 5. Adjournment

Each item on the agenda was Sam's responsibility. As she looked at the minutes of the last meeting, a crease worked its way across Samantha's brow. She was particularly bothered by the format at the top of the minutes. Immediately after the list of "Attendance," the minutes showed "Excused Members." That seemed pretty heavy-handed—akin to treating teachers like kids. But Sam did not have time to contemplate this issue, because there was a quick knocking on her door.

It was Marla Montag—Math Department chair. "Ms. Levy, we've got a problem," came Marla's urgent plea.

Samantha kept it to herself, but she always felt uncomfortable when staff referred to her as Ms. Levy; she wished they would just call her Sam. "What's the problem, Marla?"

"I know the school year has just begun, but the Math Department has already exhausted its budget. That's not even the real problem. The math textbook company isn't providing us with the workbooks. When I called the regional sales director, he told us that the workbooks would cost us an additional $4,000. What are we going to do?"

Samantha felt the blood rushing to her temples. She had no clue what to do, but one thing was for certain. It was up to her to handle this problem. "I'm not sure, but I'll look into it," came her reply. At least she felt good about one thing—she was able to think quick on her feet and give a quick response.

Marla Montag left Samantha's office with an uneasy look on her face, and Samantha didn't feel any better. She sat at her desk for about half a minute then looked out her window and picked up the phone. She dialed district math coordinator Hank Gorbo's number.

"Good morning, Hank. This is Sam." Samantha waited for a couple of seconds for a response from Mr. Gorbo, but none came.

"Sam Levy at Washington."

"Ah, good morning, Samantha!" came Hank's enthusiastic reply. "What's up?" Sam spent the next few minutes explaining the situation to Hank Gorbo. And then she asked, "How did this happen, and what can we do about it?"

Hank explained, "As you will recall, Samantha, last summer our mathematics teachers agreed on piloting this new series. We had an adoption committee made up of teachers. Unfortunately, someone made an error in the interpretation of the contract. We didn't discover the problem until the summer, and at that time it was too late. We couldn't reconvene the teacher committee because it was during summer break. So we have already been in contact with the textbook company. We have the money, and we have taken care of it."

Samantha had mixed emotions. In one sense, she felt relieved. But, in another sense . . . "Why didn't you tell me or Marla about this?"

Hank responded in a perplexed fashion, "Like I said, we took care of it. There's nothing to worry about. That's why they pay us the big bucks." He chuckled as the conversation came to a conclusion.

Sam wrote a quick e-mail to Marla explaining that everything was taken care of. Then she took a couple of moments to read her incoming mail. She scanned through her list, but one in particular caught her attention. It was from Greta McGovern, an outstanding vocal music teacher.

To: Samantha Levy
From: Greta McGovern
Re: Observation

Hi Samantha,

I know you want to come into all the probationary teachers' classrooms for observations before the end of the month. However, I'm requesting that rather than making a formal clinical observation, you permit me to do a different professional development activity. I ask you this favor for two reasons. First, I'm on the last year of my probation. Second, I've had excellent reviews these past two years.

Thanks for your consideration,

Greta McGovern
Washington High School
Vocal Music Professional

Samantha didn't know what to think. She gave a wry little smile when she noticed that Greta called her Samantha rather than her formal title. "These young teachers sure are less formal than their parents' generation." Still, she didn't know how to take Greta's request. She had to think on this one.

Many thoughts crossed her mind. She didn't know whether or not to feel any offense to the challenge of her authority. After all, teacher supervision was under the purview of the principal. But then again, Greta was such a good teacher and wonderful person; she couldn't have meant this as a challenge to Sam's authority. Another more pressing question—could this even be done? Will associate superintendent and direct supervisor of principals Bernice Pelligrini allow this? What about the collective bargaining agreement?

Samantha made a note to herself to talk to Bernice after her meeting downtown with the district assessment planning committee. And if she didn't get going now, she would be late. Today was the first time the committee would be meeting, and Samantha was the high school principal representative.

When she arrived at the conference room, which also doubled as the board of education meeting room, Samantha took a seat next to Alfonzo Tucker—principal of Longfellow Middle School—and next to Margaret Willis—principal of Alders Elementary School. The committee was chaired by Dr. Fareed Kahn—director of research and assessment. All the district curriculum coordinators made up most of the rest of the committee. Cheryl Swanson—fifth-grade teacher at Armstrong Elementary School—was the lone teacher representative. She was also a principal intern, and working on this committee helped her to meet her internship requirements.

Fareed Kahn called the meeting to order. "I'm glad you could all make it here today. We've got some very important business before us. As you heard from Superintendent Carleson's speech at the beginning of the month, the Department of Public Education is requiring that each school district assess students in grades 4, 8, 10, and 12 in order to comply with the No Child Left Behind Act. This committee's charge is to examine how our current testing system fits with the new examinations."

As Fareed continued to talk, Samantha couldn't help but look around the beautiful conference room with its cherrywood tables, executive chairs, burgundy carpeting, and masculine wallpaper. She also couldn't help but notice that Cheryl was the only teacher in the room.

She was brought back to reality when she heard Fareed ask, "Are there any questions?"

Samantha raised her hand and queried, "Will there be any more teachers on this committee? I want to make sure we get adequate representation from our teaching staff."

"Of course," Fareed interjected. "We will be putting together some working groups later this fall and winter. Several of you will be chairing these subcommittees and report back to this group with recommendations by early spring."

The committee continued to discuss the parameters, state regulations, timelines, and guiding principles for the next two hours. Then the meeting was adjourned.

As she left the conference room, Sam literally almost ran into Bernice Pelligrini. "I'm glad I ran into you," laughed Sam to the startled associate superintendent. She went on for nearly five minutes telling Bernice about Greta's request. Sam felt as if she were trying to make a sales pitch in support of Greta, even though she wasn't sure how she felt about the idea.

Bernice looked thoughtful as she listened to Samantha but began to frown when she replied. "I wish I could help you out, Sam. I really do. But if we were to bend the policy for Greta, we would have to do it for everyone. We don't want to set a precedent that might come back to haunt us someday, so we have to treat everyone the same." With that, Bernice turned to Fareed Kahn, who had been patiently waiting.

KEY POINTS

- Contemporary school governance is based upon bureaucratic models for the purpose of efficiency.
- These models do not lend themselves to democratic decision making.
- These organizational structures have remained unchanged since the beginning of the Industrial Age.

- These problems are only exacerbated with new federal and state mandates.

POINTS TO PONDER

1. How is your school governance similar and dissimilar to corporate governance and political governance?
2. What power or authority do teachers, parents, and students have in our schools?
3. Where could be places of empowerment for teachers and staff, and for parents and even students?
4. What is your school community's mimetic isomorphism?

NOTES

1. Robert Palter, ed., *The Annus Mirabilis of Sir Isaac Newton, 1666–1966* (Cambridge, MA: MIT Press, 1970), 244.

2. For a detailed analysis of the classical sciences and their impact on organizational administration, the reader is invited to read Perry R. Rettig, *Quantum Leaps in School Leadership* (Lanham, MD: Rowman & Littlefield), 2002.

3. Robert Owens, *Organizational Behavior in Education: Adaptive Leadership and School Reform* (New York: Pearson Allyn & Bacon, 2004), 83.

4. R. L. Green, *Practicing the Art of Leadership: A Problem-Based Approach to Implementing the ISLLC Standards* (Upper Saddle River, NJ: Merrill Prentice Hall, 2001), 53.

5. Peter Block, *Stewardship: Choosing Service over Self-Interest* (San Francisco: Berrett-Koehler, 1996), 8.

6. For an interesting description of the history of organizational theory, please read Teresa M. Harrison, "Designing the Post-Bureaucratic Organization: Toward Egalitarian Organizational Structure" *Australian Journal of Communication* 19(2), (1992): 14–29.

7. P. M. Blau, *The Organization of Academic Work* (New York: Wiley, 1973), in Patricia J. Gumport and Stuart K. Snydman, "The Formal Organization of Knowledge: An Analysis of Academic Structure," *The Journal of Higher Education* 73 (2002): 383.

8. According to James G. March and Johan P. Olsen,

[m]odern democracies build barriers to conflict by specializing access to institutional spheres so that many individuals and groups are excluded from many

spheres, while retaining an interpenetrated and diffuse network of popular control. Hierarchical organization, departmentalization, division of labor, specialization, and the division of responsibility are standard ways in which attention is specialized. They build cognitive and procedural buffers between groups and activities.

In *Democratic Governance* (New York: The Free Press, 1995), 79.

9. Charles Heckscher, "Defining the Post-Bureaucratic Type," in Charles Heckscher and Anne Donnellon, eds., *The Post-Bureaucratic Organization: New Perspectives on Organizational Change* (Thousand Oaks, CA: Sage, 1994), 37.

10. For a much more detailed analysis of the Weberian Model and its criticisms, Closed Systems thinking, and Classical Organizational Thought, the reader is invited to read such standard texts as Wayne Hoy and Cecil Miskel, *Educational Administration: Theory, Research, and Practice* (New York: Random House, 2004); Russ Marion, *Leadership in Education: Organizational Theory for the Practitioner* (Upper Saddle River, NJ: Merrill Prentice Hall, 2002); Robert Owens, *Organizational Behavior in Education: Adaptive Leadership and School Reform* (New York: Pearson Allyn & Bacon, 2004). In particular, Owens's work is quite thorough and readable.

11. Mihaly Csikszentmihalyi, *Flow: The Psychology of Optimal Experience* (New York: Harper Collins, 1990), 78. As evidence to this devastating phenomenon, William E. Halal cited, "It is estimated that one-fourth of employees are so abused by authority that they call in sick, limit productivity, and deliberately sabotage operations." In *The New Management: Bringing Democracy and Markets Inside Organizations* (San Francisco: Berrett-Koehler, 1998), 222.

12. Francis X. Neumann Jr., "Organizational Structures to Match the New Information-Rich Environments: Lessons from the Study of Chaos," *Public Productivity and Management Review* 21 (September 1997): 90.

13. Ibid., Owens, 90–91.

14. Ibid., 93.

15. Russ Marion, *Leadership in Education: Organizational Theory for the Practitioner* (Upper Saddle River, NJ: Merrill Prentice Hall, 2002), 73.

16. Jean Lipman-Blumen, *The Connective Edge: Leading in an Interdependent World* (San Francisco: Jossey-Bass, 1996), 61.

17. George Cheney et al., "Democracy, Participation, and Communication at Work: A Multidisciplinary Review," *Communication Yearbook* 21 (2004): 44.

18. Margaret Wheatley, *Leadership and the New Science: Learning about Organizations from an Orderly Universe* (San Francisco: Berrett-Koehler, 1994), 29.

19. William E. Halal, *The New Management: Bringing Democracy and Markets Inside Organizations* (San Francisco: Berrett-Koehler, 1998), 28.

20. Thomas Sergiovanni and Robert Starratt, *Supervision: A Redefinition* (New York: McGraw-Hill, 1993), 15.

21. Edward Greenberg, *Workplace Democracy: The Political Effects of Participation* (Ithaca, NY: Cornell University Press, 1986), 45.

22. Ibid., Rettig, 2.

23. L. Rhodes, "Connecting Leadership and Learning," A Planning Paper Developed for the *American Association of School Administrators National Center for Connected Learning* (April 1997): 16.

24. Archon Fung, *Empowered Participation: Reinventing Urban Democracy* (Princeton, NJ: Princeton University Press, 2004). Fung has studied reform efforts of the Chicago Public Schools. He noted that "Under the prior, hierarchical model of administration, the CPS . . . central offices attempted to control the operational minutiae of local activity," 69.

25. Archon Fung and Erik Olin Wright, eds., *Deepening Democracy: Institutional Innovations in Empowered Participatory Governance* (London: Verso, 2003), 18. On page 19 these authors provided further detail about the methods associated with all three of these "choices":

> In [command and control], power is invested in managers, bureaucrats, or other specialists. . . . While such experts may engage in deliberative practices among themselves, their discussions are insulated from popular participation. On the other hand, in aggregative voting the administrator will allow participation. Individual group members are permitted to vote on a variety of issues, then an algorithm such as majority rule selects a single option for the whole group. Still, invariably, it is the administrator who decides which issues make it on the agenda to receive employee consideration. Finally, strategic bargaining and negotiation is more of a power play for competing powers. Often, decisions are made based upon groups' self-interest in a win-lose bargaining process.

26. John Smyth, "The Socially Just Alternative to the 'Self-Managing School,'" in Keith Leithwood et al., eds., *International Handbook of Educational Leadership and Administration* (The Netherlands: Kluwer Academic Publishers, 1996), 1122.

27. J. Bransford, A. Brown, and A. Cocking, eds., *How People Learn: Brain, Mind, Experience, and School* (Washington, DC: National Academy Press, 1999), 120.

28. Perry R. Rettig, "Differentiated Supervision: A New Approach," *Principal* 78(3) (November 1999): 36–39.

29. Ibid., Bransford et al., 120.

30. Linda Darling-Hammond, "Target Time Toward Teachers," *Journal of Staff Development* 20 (Spring 1999): 32.

31. This is a decision-making flow chart from the Vroom-Yetton normative leadership model. From Fred Luthans, *Organizational Behavior*, 2nd edition (New York: McGraw-Hill, 1977), 458, table 1.1.

32. Richard Gorton, *School Leadership and Administration: Important Concepts, Case Studies, and Simulations* (Dubuque, IA: William C. Brown, 1987), 6.

33. Noam Chomsky, *Chomsky: On Miseducation* (Lanham, MD: Rowman & Littlefield, 2000), 16.

CHAPTER 2

It Doesn't Have to Be This Way

All modern organizations have bureaucracies. These bureaucracies help employees coordinate their daily work lives and are essential to routine actions of their organizational systems. Max Weber was concerned with arbitrary power in the hands of single individuals. He conceptualized bureaucratic structures in order to diffuse the power and authority across the entire organization.

Henri Fayol developed the structure of bureaucracies, and Frederick Taylor made the study of them a science. While bureaucracies are necessary in all modern systems, conflicts often arise in schools because of the work of the professionals within them. In the last chapter, we learned of the characteristics of bureaucracies. Let us now turn our attention to the key attributes of professions. It is well established that all professionals share a number of common characteristics:

- *Knowledge base*: Extensive training and formal knowledge.
- *Regulation and control*: Provide a service to clients and expect autonomy, but with that autonomy comes the interest of the client first.
- *Association*: Reference group orientation with other professionals.
- *Ideology*: Loyalty to the integrity of the profession and ethical standards.[1]

In common parlance, we can say that educators have a high degree of training and expertise. A professional's authority comes from this expertise. Professional educators must always be student-centered, first and foremost. In order to carry out their ethical responsibilities, teachers need autonomy to meet the idiosyncratic needs of their students.

This is where the professional-bureaucratic conflict emerges. Bureaucracies require standardization and routinization, and professions require judgment, autonomy, and flexibility. Therefore, the bureaucratic attributes of organizations are necessarily in conflict with professional attributes of organizations.[2]

This has become a systemic fact of life. In today's schools, the professionals have little power and real authority. But to some extent the professionals have brought some of this upon themselves. As the size and complexity of their organizations have increased, there has been more need for bureaucratization, and hence professionals have had less time to practice their professional obligations.

In public education, political mandates have only exacerbated this situation by creating demand for more levels of bureaucracy. Nevertheless, in the Industrial Age professional educators began to hire bureaucrats with specialization to carry out specific tasks in order to free up time for the teachers to teach. Yet the bureaucrats have been given formal authority, and the professionals have seen their power diminished.

In reality, as educators have given some responsibility to the bureaucrats, they have abdicated their power and authority. In professional organizations, the professionals should have the power and authority to make decisions. In professional bureaucracies, however, the power balance has shifted to the bureaucrats—to those removed from the service of the clients. So in public education, we have bureaucrats with more power and authority than the professional educators.

Why have professional educators given this power to others? Bureaucracies are the result of the natural tendency of people to try to control changing conditions. According to Neumann:

> The traditional organizational solution to problems . . . has been to bound, or mediate them in some fashion. So, when confronted by increasing turbulence, organizations normally respond with increasingly bureaucratic behavior by increasing structural centralization and placing greater emphasis on efficiency, standardization, and routinizaton. In the most complex environment . . . however, some finite point is reached at which, in the face of increasing environmental complexity, the capability of the hierarchical organization to further process information becomes

saturated and reaches a maximum. The increasing bureaucratic behavior is the result of a natural attempt by higher level management to increase certainty in the face of increasing uncertainty.[3]

There are a number of dubious reasons bureaucracies cannot live up to their expectations. Top-down decision making is not efficacious. "The pyramid-like organization chart . . . masks the fundamental differences in the nature and requirements of the interdependent work that must take place in it. One of the most destructive effects has been its contribution to the erroneous metaphor that organizations have 'tops' and bottoms.'"[4] A point in fact, the vast majority of Total Quality Management (TQM) programs fail because they are initiated from the top.[5]

Bureaucrats are not in a position to understand the work of the professional educator. In a most erudite manner, Rhodes stipulated, "Middle-management lives a self-fulfilling prophecy. Perceived as 'bureaucrats' operating in a rigid bureaucracy, their responsibilities are seldom aligned to the front-line problem-solving of the staff they are supposed to be supporting."[6]

Bureaucracies are purposefully configured this way. The top layers do the planning and set direction, as they are able to see the macro-picture. On the other hand, the workers carry out the plans at the micro-level.[7] One group does the thinking, and one group does the working, by design. In this postmodern era of technical specialization, however, it is impossible for the bureaucrats and top-line officials to be sufficiently knowledgeable in all aspects of the work done by those who report to them.[8]

For example, in schools a principal cannot be well versed in all content areas, technology, special education programs, ESL/bilingual, and the like. Again, the erroneous assumption is that those at the top of the organization know more than the workers.

The high degree of specialization of bureaucratic workers creates a problem of specialty. Charles Heckscher characterized three fundamental problems to what he referred to as "bureaucratic segmentation"—where people are responsible only for their own jobs.

1. *The waste of intelligence.* The first is that it systematically limits the use of intelligence by employees: the system uses only a small fraction of the capacity of its members.

2. *The formal-informal split.* The second consequence of bureaucratic segmentation is a failure effectively to control the "informal" organization.
3. *The crudeness of organization change.* The third limitation of even the best bureaucracies concerns their patterns of change and adaptation: they do not effectively manage processes over time.[9]

Rigid bureaucratic structures don't feel natural or authentic to either the workers or to the customers whom they serve. Educational systems thinker Patrick Dolan posited, "If we deliberately set out to create a model deeply antithetical to team work, we could not have done a better job than this Western orthodoxy . . . The Un-Team—It is a non-integrated structure in which groups work in silos of specialization, and individuals compete with one another for power, position, and resources."[10]

In a concurring opinion, Rhodes stated, "Unfortunately, this apparently rational model does not make intuitive sense in terms of all of the actual relationships between people's interdependent roles within the system and between the system and its ultimate customers."[11]

Finally, change in this postmodern world is complex and dynamic. It is not linear and controllable as in the past. Bureaucracies are designed to control—to maintain the status quo—and are not designed to be nimble and make the changes necessary in today's organizations.[12] Succinctly, "Too much bureaucracy makes it very difficult to change [organizations], even when change is crucial for the organization's continued success or even its survival."[13]

Yes, bureaucracies are here to stay, and we may not like it one bit. We may accept them as necessary evils. In fact, they are necessary, but we need to reconsider their purpose and the role that bureaucrats play in authoritative decision making as it relates to the professionals within our organizations.

Bureaucracies should help teachers to perform their professional duties; they should help keep the system focused and fiscally fit; they should help meet the needs of mandates, but they must not be the tail that wags the dog. Chapters 3 and 4 will attempt to explicate how educator professionals can regain their professional autonomy.

The remainder of this chapter will provide the requisite framework for this examination in two ways. First, by looking through the lens of

Critical Theory, we will dispel the myths of the need for command and control of traditional organizations and of the purported empowerment of the Human Relations Approach. Second, we will explore the postmodern approaches of Open Systems Theories.

CRITICAL LENS

> People of discretion. Experts. I do not like experts. They are our jailors. I despise experts more than anyone on earth. . . . They solve nothing! They are servants of whatever system hires them. They perpetuate it. When we are tortured, we shall be tortured by experts. When we are hanged, experts will hang us. . . . When the world is destroyed, it will be destroyed not by madmen but by the sanity of its experts and the superior ignorance of its bureaucrats.[14]

These lines of a Soviet scientist in John le Carré's novel *The Russian House* capture the essence of workers' deepening frustrations to those individuals who have authority over them. This is the type of emotion entwined in Critical Theory. Unbeknownst to many administrative practitioners in our schools, there is a body of research called Critical Theory.

This research has remained on the fringe of administrative preparation programs because of its revolutionary bent and because of its lack of prescription. More succinctly, it's too radical with no perceived practical application for school leaders.

Critical Theory is just that. It's a theory (or better—a way of thinking) that is critical of the way things are. Critical theorists question everything. They question the status quo, power and authority, even their own motivation. They look to truly empower workers. "Critical theory exposes abuses by elites and explores alternatives, more democratic, and egalitarian models of organization."[15]

Proponents of Critical Theory desire bosses and workers alike to examine the status quo, to examine our assumptions of power relationships and of decision-making protocols, and to examine what we take for granted in our institutions.[16] In order to take a critical look at these assumptions, procedures, and relationships people need to enter processes of substantive dialogue. They must be allowed to express dissenting opinions without fear of subtle reprisal.

Famous for his authorship of *A People's History of the United States*, Howard Zinn wrote, "The problem with free speech in the United States is not with the fact of access, but with the degree of it. There is some access to dissident views, but these are pushed into a corner. And there is some departure in the mainstream press from government policy, but it is limited and cautious."[17]

A low-level employee needs to be secure when challenging power and authority in their institution. During the Industrial Age, management controlled with an iron fist. Everyone knew where they stood. The shift to the modern era of Human Relations Approaches has made the power dynamic more difficult to see. According to Jermier:

> Contemporary mechanisms of control are often unobtrusive. . . . Although organizational theorists have long acknowledged that processes of control are integral to the way organizations operate there are reasons to believe that we have entered a new age in which the forms of control being used are more insidious and widely misunderstood.[18]

Therefore, the manipulation of Human Resources Management is unethical and tricks workers into feeling they are empowered, when in fact, they are not.[19] Workers are asked to work on committees that carry out the vision of their supervisors. Yet they have no say in the vision. They set their goals, but the goals are from an allotment approved by administration. They are mentored into the ways of the system and told, "This is the way we do things around here." They become corporate clones with group-think. Perhaps the greatest irony is the suburbanization of organizational culture.

Employees have worked hard to get and maintain these jobs. They are compensated well and have very good health and retirement benefits. In other words, they have become too comfortable, with too much to lose, to speak out against the group-think. When a subordinate voices dissidence, they could lose everything. So they keep quiet and don't verbalize their objections. This inaction is repeated every day in every department. Workers have become victims of their own success.

To summarize, Critical Theory asks people to question power relationships and motives of those making the decisions. While Critical Theory not only criticizes the status quo, it also looks to truly empower employees through democratic processes. In the words of Maxim Voronov and Peter Coleman, "Critical theory seeks to expose instances in which ideology constrains and oppresses certain groups while giving unfair advantage to others and to create more democratic workplaces."[20]

Critical Theory has taught us to be wary of hierarchical structures. There is little doubt that hierarchies and their subsequent bureaucracies have taken on a life of their own—a life that is choking out the life of the creative people who populate them. Furthermore, Critical Theory demands that those in power continually reflect upon their actions and policies to evaluate both their purposes and their effects.

Critical Theory has direct application to school systems, as well. Two fundamental areas need to be explored: process and decision making, and curriculum and classroom. District and building administrators control information and make final decisions with little or no real input from teachers. Meanwhile, the central office bureaucrats set direction, create expectations, and inspect the professionals' progress toward those expectations. When they cut budgets, administrators make decisions with "patriarchal compassion."

School personnel find themselves operationally led by innumerable impersonal policies. Staff development at times has little to do with individual classroom instruction, and teacher supervision and evaluation are often perfunctory. Curricular choices are decided by curriculum experts at central offices or at state-level agencies and adopted by school board members, all of whom are far removed from the classroom. Likewise, "shared decision-making" protocols tend to be paternal. Teachers "feel" empowered but are not truly empowered, as their administrators make the final decisions.[21]

This statement might seem over the top; however, it is quite likely that the reader has served on committees where the group has made a decision only to be overturned by the administration. It should also be noted that these educator committees typically only can make recommendations—they have no real authority. This is very routine, and it has created terrible morale issues among professional educators.

There is an alternative, however. Democratic decision-making processes and dialogue are central features to any school system that chooses to provide a critical praxis and dialectic as defined by Paulo Freire.[22] Critical dialogue is the vehicle for practitioners to become aware of their condition, their promise, and how to get there.[23] Viviane Robinson elucidated how this is to be accomplished:

> Participants in a problem-solving discourse must be committed to three discourse values. The first, that of respect, ensures . . . fair opportunity to speak, to challenge or to continue any line of inquiry, to express one's feeling and to be in general unconstrained in one's dealing with the other parties in the discourse. The second discourse value is that of commitment to valid information. It involves commitment to the conduct of discourse in ways that increase the chances of detection of error in one's own and others' claims about the nature of the problem and how to solve it . . . they welcome rather than discourage different perspectives. . . . The third value, that of commitment to the process and outcomes of dialogue . . . involves being motivated to expend the intellectual and emotional effort required until all parties can proclaim to each other and to third parties that they have a solution that is the best they can construct, given their mutually agreed constraints on the problem.[24]

In other words, the professional workplace must offer a time and a place for teachers to have honest and open dialogue. Teachers must feel free to express themselves, to have transparent dialogue and come to a reasoned conclusion together.

Teachers and their students must also use Critical Theory concepts in their classrooms. As it stands in our contemporary classrooms across the country, students—in reality—are treated as passive sponges soaking up knowledge. They have very little say in where they are placed, what they learn, how they learn, and how their progress is to be evaluated.

Paulo Freire noted, "The more students work at storing the deposits entrusted to them, the less they develop the critical consciousness which would result from their intervention in the world as transformers of that world. The more completely they accept the passive role imposed on them, the more they tend simply to adapt to the world as it is and to the fragmented view of reality deposited in them."[25] This is to say, students need an opportunity to practice the value of democracy, both the autonomy and the responsibility associated with it.

The National Research Council stipulated, "The factory model affect[s] the design of curriculum, instruction, and assessment in schools."[26] "Rather than standardizing curriculum, materials, and pedagogy, individual teachers and school sites must be given the opportunity to react to the particular needs of their unique students."[27]

Specifically, what are teachers to do? Beyer and Bigelow give us some insight. "Effective teachers reflect critically on the moral, political, social, and economic dimensions of education. This requires an understanding of the multiple contexts in which schools function, an appreciation of diverse perspectives on educational issues, and a commitment to democratic forms of interaction."[28]

Furthermore, according to Bigelow, "One function of the school curriculum is to celebrate the culture of the dominate and to ignore or scorn the culture of the subordinate groups. . . . Students . . . can *create* [emphasis in original] knowledge, not simply absorb it from higher authorities." William Bigelow went on to state:

> I do not think that our classrooms can ever be exact models of the kind of participatory democracy we would like to have characterize the larger society. If teachers' only power were to grade students, that would be sufficient to sabotage classroom democracy. However, classrooms can offer students experiences and understandings that counter, and critique, the lack of democracy in the rest of their lives. In the character of student interactions the classroom can offer a glimpse of certain features of an egalitarian society.[29]

POSTMODERN IDEOLOGY IN QUANTUM REALITY

A quick historical note is appropriate here. The classical Newtonian model of management, with its bureaucratic hierarchy, took hold across American institutions during the Industrial Age. The machine was the metaphor, and its remnants stay with us in terms of organizational structure, communication patterns, policy development and implementation, Theory X motivation principles, and curriculum and pedagogy. In a particularly poignant fashion, Fritjof Capra explained,

> [s]ocial thought in the late nineteenth and early twentieth centuries was greatly influenced by positivism, a doctrine formulated by the social philosopher Auguste Comte. Its assertions include the insistence that

the social sciences should search for general laws of human behavior. ... It is evident that the positivist framework is patterned after classical physics. Indeed, Auguste Comte, who introduced the term, "sociology," first called the scientific study "social physics." The major schools of thought in early-twentieth-century sociology can be seen as attempts at emancipation from the positivist straitjacket.[30]

A very different second wave of Closed Systems thinking followed in the 1960s and 1970s. (While the new model was theorized in the two or three decades before it, the model was not truly practiced in organizations until our society was ready for the Age of Aquarius.) This was the Human Relations Approach. This more *humane* model focused primarily on making workers happy in their work, yet the purpose was still to maximize effectiveness.

Some remnants of the Human Relations model include open concept schools, middle schools, SRI reading kits, self-paced instruction, nongraded classes, team-based staff development, and the like. The idea behind the Human Relations Approach was that in order to make employees more efficient workers, they needed to be happy workers.

Employee Assistance Programs were initiated, teacher supervision became much more ephemeral, and staff development activities focused on employee emotional and social needs. The role of school leaders was to create a climate whereby staff would be emotionally satisfied, all in order to make them more productive.

Not everyone was happy with this laid-back approach to teaching and learning and its management style. The country elected a new President in Ronald Reagan, who ran on a back-to-basics and accountability platform. The pendulum of school administration had swung back in the 1980s to a neoclassical model.

This third wave of Closed Systems thinking has left remnants, as well. In fact, it is the model most identifiable with our current systems. This model has brought with it more standardization in terms of teaching, testing, and curriculum. Management systems now provide for more site-based management, parental choice, and zero-based budgeting. Competition is in, and accountability is the mantra.

But behind the scenes a rekindled yet new movement has been lurking. It is Open Systems thinking with a renewed interest in science—

albeit the newer sciences. This new postmodern view of organizations as natural systems is antipositivistic, nondeterministic, and operates with an ecological or jungle-like metaphor. It doesn't subscribe to the notion that there is a linear way to understand problems and a purely rational way to administrate.

Rather, this original movement born out of the 1960s believes that there is multiple and complex causation to most problems, that most decisions are not made with complete knowledge of all variables, and that organizations and their leaders are dramatically influenced by the contexts of their environments. Open Systems theorists view their institutions through a holistic lens and consider these systems as alive.

Like previous models, Open Systems theories arose in reaction to the shortcomings of their predecessors. "While alluring in their simplicity, mechanical concepts of school change run counter to the experience of most educators, who have learned to view all activity in schools as deeply human, subject to the baffling complexity that permeates most human endeavors."[31] Still, all Open Systems theories have a few things in common.

First, they hold that few simple cause-effect relationships exist within real-life systems. Effects are often far removed—in time and space—from their multiple causes. Second, top-down hierarchies, even though designed for efficiency, are ineffective and inefficient.

Finally, human organizations should be considered dynamic living systems, unlike the rigid Closed Systems models that fail to interact with their environments. Whereas Closed Systems thinking took its cues from Newtonian physics, Open Systems thinking learned its lessons from the newer sciences, like quantum physics, ecology, biology, and chaos theory.[32]

Just what is quantum physics? Quantum physics can best be defined as a "statistical theory that deals with probabilities."[33] It looks at the interconnectedness of the universe at the subatomic level. Its language is the more intuitive and qualitative mathematics of patterns and relationships. Perhaps a few brief theoretical examples from the quantum sciences and one from the other newer sciences will help to illustrate.

Bell's Theorem is also known as nonlocal causality. This experiment was conceptualized mathematically before it was verified in the laboratory. What John Bell discovered was the idea that you could pair together two electrons. Once they were paired together, you could separate them at macroscopic distances. After they were separated, the experimenter/observer could change the spin of one of the electrons.

In a most interesting twist, the other electron would instantaneously change its spin in corresponding fashion even though it could not *see* the other electron. Physicist Victor Mansfield and Jungian analyst J. Marvin Spiegelman explained, "Surprisingly, *this instantaneous interaction or dependency occurs without any information or energy exchange between regions A and B* [emphasis in original]. The effect occurs without a definite cause—a truly acausal connection.... We understand this interconnectedness in terms of effects propagating faster than the speed of light."[34]

How could this be? We are trapped by our limited, classical thinking. We know of no other way to understand. It is *apparent* that the two objects are separate, but that is the trap. The two objects are not necessarily two objects, or separate. They are interconnected, or one object. "It is a quantum loophole through which physics admits the necessity of a unitary vision."[35] Interconnectedness and relationships are the centerpiece to this quantum world, and communication is the glue to these relationships. There is not an observer separate from the observed.

Two other important quantum discoveries may help to illustrate newer Open Systems thinking. The Principle of Complementarity and Heisenberg's Uncertainty Principle are two theories that work together. Niels Bohr created the Principle of Complementarity whereby light shows dualistic attributes, both particles and waves. Not one or the other, but both, and both simultaneously. Our Newtonian way of thinking has led us to believe that atoms can only be particles or only wave-like at any given moment, not both simultaneously. In reality, they are both particles and wavelike concurrently.

Bohr found no problem with this natural duality. He coined the word "complementarity" to explain that nature needs both sides of the same coin. They are different but not separate. Both need one another—they complement each other. However, we can only see one side at a time, and that's the Heisenberg Uncertainty Principle.

In quantum physics, the scientists could determine the location of an atom, but not its velocity. Or they could measure its speed, but not where it's located. Both sides complement one another, but we can never be fully certain to all its aspects. Our quick snapshot views of complex systems only allow us to see parts, but not the whole.

Schrödinger's Cat is a thought experiment that adds yet another lesson from the quantum sciences. Austrian physicist Erwin Schrödinger designed an imaginary experiment wherein a live cat is placed inside a metal box. The box is enclosed in such a fashion that no one can see what is happening inside. A mechanism triggers the release of either a food pellet or deadly cyanide gas.

Now the conundrum. Through mathematical figuring Schrödinger showed that after the trigger released either the food or the poison the cat is both dead and alive at the same time; that is, until the observer opens the box. At the instant of observation, the cat is then observed as either alive or dead, and the alternate chance is gone forever. This thought experiment shows that the observer impacts the observed. In other words, we will impact any situation by our mere presence.

From Bell's Theorem, the Principle of Complementarity, and the Heisenberg Uncertainty Principle, we learn of the unifying dynamic of nature. We are not separate; we are inextricably interconnected. Isolating by measurement of individual parts does not give us a better understanding of the whole. The whole can only be understood by examining the entire system in a unified fashion.

This is in contrast to the lessons learned from the conventional sciences. In the past we learned of the importance of reductionism, objectivity, control, replication, and prediction. However, Margaret Wheatley captured the lessons from the new sciences with "Shifts in Scientific and Organizational Thinking":

Shift 1: From the parts to the whole.
Shift 2: From understanding processes rather than structures.
Shift 3: To understanding that the universe is a web of relationships, constantly shifting and growing.
Shift 4: Towards the realization that we can never know reality absolutely or predict anything.[36]

Chaos theory and the science of complexity provide us yet additional insights into the mysteries of dynamic systems. Classical thermodynamics taught us that a system's optimal level is equilibrium. In other words, all systems strive for equilibrium or homeostasis.

Because we have been such good students of the classical sciences, we have learned to strive for equilibrium in our organizations—the hallmark of bureaucracies and standardization. We wish to maintain consistency and control where everything is static. However, in chaos theory we learn that equilibrium is a state of entropy—the state where systems begin to die.

When a system becomes static, it does not create or evolve, so it dies. Yet as Capra posited, "In the new science of complexity . . . we learn that nonequilibrium is a source of order."[37] We so desperately want to maintain consistency and control, where everything is in a state of equilibrium. When a system is at equilibrium, it cannot change, entropy takes over, and the natural system dies. On the other hand, when a system fluctuates and makes changes, it *appears* to be in disorder or chaos. But this place between order and chaos is what scares us the most.

This is called the bifurcation point; it's where the system can either reorganize into a higher level or die. We're mostly afraid of the death part! Education is clearly seeing unmistakable signs of bifurcation and chaos as we move further and further from equilibrium. The signs are the movements toward charter schools, school choice, the standards movement, more stringent teacher licensure, high-stakes testing, and the quintessential back-to-basics movement.

As has been mentioned earlier, human organizations are not closed systems like machines; rather, they are open systems like nature. Margaret Wheatley explained, "Open systems don't sit quietly by as their energy dissipates. They don't seek equilibrium. Quite the opposite. To stay viable, open systems maintain a state of non-equilibrium, keeping the system off balance so that it can change and grow."[38]

What might *appear* to be disorder or chaos may really be an underlying order. What the observer needs to do is allow for the order to appear. We humans are only able to see a small part of the system in terms of space and time. We do not see the system in its entirety. We are not trained to do so.

There are two primary lessons we can take from chaos theory back to our schools. First, people need to be patient when things appear to be chaotic. We need to take the time to let patterns develop, and to look over the entire system for these patterns to emerge.

The term "space" refers to the entire organization. We must look beyond our own departments or individual classrooms to see the interconnections and relationships.[39] The term "time" refers to taking more than the typical snapshot of time in which we make our observations. That's why so much of what we see appears to be chaotic. A glimpse of living things can appear to be chaotic. But over time and space, patterns or themes tend to emerge and show themselves. Order can come out of chaos.

The second lesson from chaos theory is no less important. "A small fluctuation may start an entirely new evolution that will drastically change the whole behavior of the macroscopic system. The analogy with social phenomena . . . is inescapable."[40] That is to say that apparently insignificant issues can create major changes. One person or small event can indeed make an enormous impact.

If we were to reflect on the lessons that we can take away from quantum physics and the other newer sciences, we would discover:

- *All parts of the organization and all people within the organization are interconnected.* Building relationships is critical to our work within these organizations. "We have finally come to see the world as a single, albeit complicated, system, one immense set of interrelated pieces."[41]

  Communication is critical to the unification of the system/organization. "Managerial work today is less about wielding power than about coping with dependence . . . managers are put into a far more complex web of interaction with influential others than any organization chart can suggest," according to Harvard University professor of business J. Kotter.[42]

- *It is often very difficult to draw direct linear causation in these complex networks.* Acausal and nonlinear effects most often rule the day. This will have correlating impact upon our typical rational decision-making strategies. We usually apply simple rational decision-making processes to nonrational issues. (This notion will be covered in more detail later in this chapter.)

- *There is a duality in nature and in all people.* While we may acknowledge this duality, we can only see one side at a time. We need to reframe our perceptions of problems and of people; we need to move from "either/or" thinking to a "both/and" vision. When we create a duality without the complementarity in our understanding of organizations and their people, we limit ourselves from seeing the full picture, and we subsequently attempt to solve problems with simplistic solutions.

- *Objectivity is virtually impossible.* The very nature of observing directly impacts the system. Our participation in the system really only permits subjective analysis of the human dynamic organization. Jungian analyst Victor Mansfield and physicist Marvin Spiegelman reasoned: "We must now abandon our servitude to strict causality, the idea that all events have some well-defined set of causes and that the same initial conditions always generate the same effects.

    "Now we must learn to appreciate that although nature is structured and lawful, it is acausal."[43] And as nature is inherently subjective, our intuitions are reasonable insights to accept and even to encourage in our employees. Since natural phenomena are subjective by nature, rather than objective, prediction and replication are inherently futile and impossible to do effectively.

- *Very often there is an underlying order embedded or emerging from apparent chaos.* By visualizing organizations over time and space, we can see the patterns and themes of order. Snapshots provide only a chaotic view. Systems can survive only if they do change. We may not feel comfortable with the lack of control, but it's a control that we really never had in the first place.

    We should embrace these fluctuations and changes, as they are the process in which order becomes restored. Very often, change comes from disorder or chaos. The critical point where a system can either jump to a higher level of organization or fall into true disarray and die is called the bifurcation point.[44]

- *Information is the lifeblood of all organizations.* Without information flowing freely throughout the organization, people cannot make wise decisions. We need to stop holding back information because we feel people cannot handle the truth.

Numerous scholars have shown us how we can apply these lessons to our organizations.[45] The new sciences tell us that in natural systems, apparent chaos and disorder might actually be a new order unfolding. The very act of control and demand for homeostasis might actually harm or even kill the organization.

At times we might need to allow the chaos to arise and the new order to unfold. But we must take a system-wide view.[46] Thus, we must avoid the compulsion to control and make quick decisions at times. Sometimes it is necessary to live with the uneasiness and allow the process to unfold.

In terms of how we operate our organizations, experimentation and risk-taking are important.[47] Many Fortune 500 companies set aside good portions of their budgets to invest in trials or pilots that allow for them to experiment on the side. You seldom will see that in the public and nonprofit sectors.

Charter schools may be just such a tool in public education. Teachers should be allowed opportunities to explore with their curriculum and pedagogy. Most importantly, they need time to let their experimentations develop. Even further, we need to encourage other voices and perceptions into decision making.

Francis Neumann further explained not only that nonlinear models are most appropriate for governmental bodies, but that chaos should actually be used as a tool for dynamic growth. In his description of L. D. Kiel's work, Neumann posited,

> Kiel wrote that public administration traditionally has focused on incremental or equilibrium models, which do not account for instances when dramatic wholesale change can occur. He suggested that nonequilibrium processes appear to be more descriptive of the interactions of democratic societies, in which the political process brings external energy into the system and drives it far from equilibrium. It is the nonlinear process that allows the system to incorporate change within itself and to adapt to changing external environments. Kiel also suggested that agents can purposefully force change in organizations by energetically driving those organizations toward the points of chaotic thresholds. For example, he cited the situation in which Japanese executives intentionally drive their organizations to chaotic symmetry breaks. "Organizational upheaval is seen as positive. It creates instability, chaos, and the potential for genuine qualitative change."[48]

The notion that our systems can be controlled and maintained at a state of equilibrium is erroneous. The tighter we try to squeeze our fist of control, the more the actual control or power oozes out between our fingers. We operate our organizations as if they were tightly controlled systems, but again, that control is elusive. Human organizations operate more like loosely coupled systems. "Today's large organizations are disaggregating into loosely connected clusters of autonomous business units."[49]

Rhodes explained the false sense of power within the reality of loosely coupled systems. "Note that power and control in each world [the worlds of the planners and doers] is relatively meaningless since, in actuality, each remains relatively powerless to affect the system's results as long as they remain disconnected from each other."[50]

Proponents of loosely coupled systems believe that organizations are not nearly as tightly organized and managed in practice as one would believe by looking at flow charts and organizational charts. Therefore, we need to create organizational models that embrace broader involvement and participation, rather than try to control it.

Furthermore, the formal organization and administration do not significantly impact methods of classroom instruction. For example, no matter what the principal or district demands in terms of lesson plans and curriculum guides, teachers will still close their doors and teach how and what they want.

Likewise, teachers have little direct instructional communication with their colleagues. For instance, despite our attempts to control the curriculum, it is most likely that any given teacher does not know precisely what their neighbor teacher is teaching at any given moment, and they certainly are unfamiliar with what is being taught by teachers at different grade levels or academic areas. This is the reality, yet we tend to communicate to our public that our curriculum is a tightly controlled structure.

But being loosely coupled is an extremely important feature in professional organizations. Professionals often operate through their intuitions and experiences. They need to be allowed to have professional autonomy. This supports the notion that educating is an art, and it allows the educator to use the "teachable moment" with discretion.

Loosely coupled systems (see table 2.1) allow for flexibility and professional autonomy, and they allow for change to take place in rela-

Table 2.1. Karl Weick's Loosely Coupled Systems Pros and Cons

Pro	Con
1. Allows sections of an organization to persist and evolve independently of one another.	1. Units aren't pressured to discontinue nonproductive practices.
2. Small, loosely coupled units are more sensitive to environmental demands.	2. This may subject the system to the whim of energy-draining fads.
3. Allows local adaptation to local environmental conditions.	3. May hinder the diffusion of local changes that could benefit the entire system.
4. Isolated units can experiment with novelty without committing the entire system to those innovations.	4. Looseness may inhibit the diffusion of experiments that are productive.
5. Allows the organization to isolate problems or breakdowns.	5. Isolated units may receive little help from the rest of the organization.
6. Loosely coupled units are self-sufficient, thus encouraging more flexible response to uncertain environments.	6. Self-sufficiency means that units may be on their own in hostile situations.
7. It may be cheaper to run a loosely coupled system than to provide the expensive coordinating structures needed for a tight system.	7. The trade-off is a loss of control.

tive isolation to the rest of the system. The flip side to these positive attributes of loosely coupled systems is that change takes a great deal of time over the entire organization, and individuals have less control over the change process than they may wish or expect. Russ Marion succinctly summarized the seven pros and cons of Weick's loosely coupled systems model.[51]

For school leaders, be they department chairs or administrators, the lessons from loosely coupled systems theory are important. As we learned with chaos theory, we must fight the compulsion to control every aspect of the institution. The power we have *over* people is a misnomer. The power we have *with* people is more the reality.

We must encourage and support professional autonomy within the smallest local units of our organizations and do all we can to build connections among these units and provide them with all information available. Finally, we must resist the temptation to standardize and routinize all aspects of the curriculum and of pedagogy. Standardization and routinization are attempts to maintain equilibrium, and in professional systems—like all natural systems—they are a recipe for failure.

In chapter 1, we talked about the Closed Systems approach to understanding people and to subsequent principles of motivation. McGregor's Theory X neatly expresses these beliefs that people are inherently lazy and not responsible, and that it is the role of the administration to supervise, to make clear expectations, and to inspect employees' work toward these expectations—in short, to motivate their workers. Theory X is a congruent model for Closed Systems thinking; Theory X is not a congruent model for Open Systems thinking.

McGregor, however, provided a model to understand the motivational principles associated with Open Systems thinking. He termed this model "Theory Y." Theory Y is literally the antithesis of Theory X. Theory Y stipulates that people are inherently good, goal-oriented, and they seek responsibility. Further, people are naturally cooperative and hardworking. In short, they are self-motivated.

When we see examples of people who are lazy and competitive, it is not because of innate attributes; rather it is due to a heavy-handed, bureaucratic system that has beaten them down to a point that they are no longer self-motivated. They have given up and begin to say, "Just tell me what you want me to do." The implications for leaders are clear. We need to start by trusting our professional colleagues.

We need to enter a dialogue with them to find what motivates them and to treat them as autonomous individuals. We need to stop feeling responsible to motivate them. We need to support the work that they find enriching and provide them with a sense of self-efficacy.

Many people have a vested interest in maintaining the status quo. In the past, as school systems became larger, more complex, and greater expectations put upon them, administration felt a need to control. Edward Greenberg captured this concern:

> The historic political problem internal to the enterprise, therefore, has been the struggle over the control of the work force and how to get it to work willingly, energetically, and smoothly. Reforms and reorganization efforts such as Taylorism, scientific management, humanistic supervision, personnel management, and the like were originated for this purpose.[52]

Likewise, Teresa Harrison claimed, "Research has typically assumed that concepts and categories articulated by classical theory, such as 'supervisors,' 'subordinates,' and even the entire top-down structure we know as bureaucratic hierarchy, are natural and necessary features of organization. . . . bureaucratic hierarchy continues to be treated as fundamental to our everyday notion of organization—a taken-for-granted feature of organizational life."[53] But research on employee satisfaction for their institutions' management systems indicate a need for change.[54]

Maintaining management practices the way they are has numerous drawbacks. There are several key features of bureaucratic hierarchies that require today's leaders to relegate this industrial management model to the realm of antiquity:

- *Inappropriate metaphor*: The machine metaphor no longer, if it ever did, fits the way human organizations actually work. It also treats people inhumanely. "Capable, well-intentioned people working in corporations, governments, and other institutions are trapped in outmoded hierarchical structures."[55]
- *Bureaucracies are not efficient*: "Bureaucracy is a bad word . . . often for quite justifiable reasons. It is blamed with inefficiency, inflexibility, and general inhumanity."[56] Likewise, "There is growing evidence that this form of organizational structure is no longer as efficient or as productive as it once was."[57]
- *Bureaucracies tend to suppress creativity*: Inside these complex organizations, the workers are not able to express their unique ideas. Standardization and rigidity do not adequately permit creativity. "It is now well established that the rigid hierarchies to be found in many state organizations are inefficient. One reason why this is so is that hierarchies tend to suppress the insights and knowledge of those at the middle and the bottom."[58]
- *Hierarchies create adversarial relations*: Bureaucratic hierarchies are not only functionally archaic, but they create unnecessary relational disorder, as well. "The central operating assumption has been the materialistic assertion that labor and management exist in a necessarily adversarial relationship."[59]
- *Bureaucracies are antithetical to teamwork*: With a division of labor and poor communication strategies, our systems do not facilitate good collaboration. "It is only gradually being understood that certain bureaucratic features like a narrow division of labor

and the vertical ordering of titles and authority are not hospitable to teamwork."[60]
- *Decision making is done far from the locus of the action*: Ultimate authority in hierarchies is placed with those on the top—those furthest from the work of service to the customers. "The bulk of useful knowledge lies unused among employees at the bottom of the firm and scattered outside its walls among customers, suppliers, and other groups—while most decisions are made by executives at the top."[61]
- *Bureaucracies are not responsive to change*: Organizational bureaucracies are designed to maintain the status quo and not for evolution. "Bureaucracies implement policies and learn how to do so from their experience, but they are limited in the degree to which they can make structural changes in response to their own idiosyncratic experience."[62]

Bureaucratic hierarchies clearly have their critical limitations. These issues range from being unable to deliver the pragmatism for which they were designed to serving as dehumanizing places to work. And for the purpose of this book, bureaucratic hierarchies are not congruent with our country's foundational democratic principles, as we will explore in the subsequent chapter. Well-renowned political analyst for CNN and the *Washington Post* Fareed Zakaria reported, "Historically, unchecked centralization has been the enemy of liberal democracy."[63]

SAM GOES TO WASHINGTON

With the charter bus doors opening, Samantha Levy and her Washington High School field trip students embarked on an experience that was sure to have lasting impact on them for years to come. The students were to gain memories of their senior year class trip to their nation's capital. They would learn as much about the stunning beauty and architecture of Washington, DC, as they would about how the nation conducts its business. Principal Levy was about to learn much about her own leadership and to start a process of deep introspection that would change how she leads her school in the future.

This biannual excursion began with an e-mail sent by Social Studies Department chair Jose Perez to all faculty, requesting chaperones. While Samantha had been to the capital many times before, she had never gone on a field trip there. Feeling a need to get out of the office, she told Jose she'd like to join the group. Besides, Washington, DC, was world renowned for the blossoming of the cherry trees in the spring.

Besides Jose and Samantha, three other staff members and five parents agreed to chaperone. Samantha was happy that Jose was extremely well organized and took care of all the tedious preparations and requisite permission forms and reservations. One aspect of the trip was left to Samantha. Senator Catherine Beyers was Sam's college roommate, and it was Samantha's responsibility to set up a time for the senator to meet with the students. Although the two coeds had kept in touch only through the occasional birthday card or holiday newsletter, both looked forward to getting reacquainted.

The charter bus doors opened, and Samantha was greeted by the open arms of Senator Beyers. They were almost pushed aside as the stream of students flooded the mall—in all its captivating glory. The chaperones eventually were able to collect the young sightseers to a grassy slope. The senator welcomed them to her life.

"Good morning and welcome to your nation's capital," Senator Beyers began. "I don't know if you are aware, but your principal and I were college roommates." The students looked at her, then over to Samantha Levy, and then back to the senator. Incredulous looks covered their faces.

The senator continued, "Before we take a walking tour, I'd like to give you a brief history of the area. I will be very brief, as I know Mr. Perez did a wonderful job in teaching you these facts." Senator Beyers was brief and interjected a few comments about the area that would not be found in the history texts. A few of the more extroverted students asked a number of questions, and ten minutes later the groups broke up to take their tours. Samantha and Catherine walked together with a group of six students, and they caught up on old times.

"Listen, Sam. I have to go to a committee hearing over the next two hours. I'll meet you in the Rotunda after, and we'll continue the guided tour." With that Senator Beyers left Samantha and her young charges. It was time for an early lunch—a box lunch provided by a local catering shop. Still, it was better than the lunches the kids were used to getting.

Student Council president Willis Davidson startled Samantha with a question. "Ms. Levy, why is it that everyone in our country says they believe in democracy, yet the one place we teach it, school, is not a democracy? I mean, I have heard teachers say, 'This is not a democracy.' I'm inspired by being here. I'm thinking about going into politics. But schools are where we are taught about democracy, but they are the antithesis of democracy."

Samantha choked on her apple. She wasn't sure what startled her more—the substance of Willis's question, or that he used the word "antithesis." Before she could respond, Elizabeth rejoined.

"Yeah. I mean, teachers don't 'walk the talk.' They talk about our founding principles, yet we don't get to see them in action."

Kyle was right on her heels. "I know that we can't have the students vote on everything, but where do we get representation?"

Jose Perez was seated nearby. He not only served as Social Studies Department chair, but he also was Student Council advisor. While Samantha was wiping her mouth with a brown paper napkin, he decided to intercede. "Kyle, students do have a voice; they are represented through their Student Council."

"I'm glad you said that, Mr. Perez," Willis replied. "I do think that Student Council gives us the opportunity to experience democratic decision making. But it's not the same. I mean, we focus on issues that aren't all that important. We talk about prom, student fundraising and special events, awards, and things like that. But we don't talk about the big issues of the curriculum, the budget, personnel issues, and policies."

Samantha was feeling on edge with this conversation. "But schools aren't democracies, Willis. Our community, through their democratically elected board, hires a superintendent who in turn hires other professionals to carry out the responsibilities of teaching. These are highly trained adults. I mean no disrespect by this, but high schoolers are not adults, nor are they trained in teaching."

As she saw the depressed look cover Willis's face, she felt like she had become one of those people she never felt she would become. Willis looked like he had just learned that he would have to resign to his fate of no control, as if he had gotten beaten, as if there were no hope. "I'm sorry, Willis. You bring up a worthwhile topic here. Certainly, there have to be limits to student participation, but I think some of us could continue the discussion when we get back home next week."

"Count me in," said Elizabeth. "But only if we really get to do something. I mean, I don't want to just go in so we *feel* like we are being listened to. I mean, I really want to be able to make a difference. We've had teachers say they will let us make choices, but when it really comes down to it, we don't have choices. So we just give up."

"I hear you, Elizabeth," Samantha replied. "I can't make you any promises except that I promise to listen and to talk."

With that said, people began to move around and move on to other subjects. The day continued with Senator Beyers leading them through the capital. They even got to see a committee in session. Tomorrow they would see the White House, the Pentagon, and do other sightseeing.

Jose had earlier told Samantha that after dinner she would have the evenings free to herself. The only caveat was that she needed to keep her cell phone on. This gave Samantha and Catherine a chance to get together for some more personal time. At 7:00, Samantha took a cab over to Catherine's apartment.

Catherine had already prepared a plate of a splendid variety of cheese and crackers along with a chilled bottle of a red Cabernet.

"What a fantastic little place you have here, Catherine. The cheese plate is delightful. But I'll have to pass on the wine. It wouldn't look good for the principal to go back with alcohol on her breath."

"I hadn't even thought of that, Sam. Sorry. How about some sparkling water?"

After they caught up with each other's lives, Samantha told of her lunch chat with the Student Council students. She concluded with, "They had me, Cath. I told them the standard line, but I had never really considered why we do what we do. I just went with what we've always done. But I wasn't satisfied with my answer, and I know they weren't. What do you think?"

"Well, of course, there have to be clear boundaries between what are the issues kids can participate in and what are the responsibilities that must fall onto the shoulders of the paid professionals. Maybe you can start there with your discussion with the students. Issues that the educators will be held accountable for must be their responsibility. But, again, democracies are for adults. Are the adults in your building treated with respect to democratic values?"

"I don't understand. What do you mean?" asked Samantha.

"I don't know. How are decisions made in your building? Who has final authority in all decisions? What role do teachers and staff have in decisions and visioning?"

"They have quite a bit of professional autonomy in how they teach. They have a variety of committees that report to the Site Council. They set their own department budgets and do peer evaluations. I think they have a lot of decision-making authority."

Catherine replied, "What if one of their committees decides on a particular approach to teaching or of the use of a certain book, and you disagree with them? Who wins? When it comes to setting the budgets, do you give each department a set amount, and they decide within those parameters, or do they get the whole school budget to work with? Are their peer evaluations more observations or evaluations? Do they set the goals for the school?"

"Of course, they set the goals for the school." Samantha tried not to sound agitated or defensive. "I mean, each year the Site Council establishes three or four school-wide goals. We always have a goal for improving test scores, one for technology, one for at-risk or underachieving students, and one for a particular curricular area. It is my role to evaluate the teachers. In fact, they don't want to evaluate each other. In other words, they don't want to make personnel decisions. I give their department a predetermined budget amount based upon previous needs and incorporating cuts or adds as appropriate. And, face it, I have to have ultimate authority in all decisions that come out of my building. So if the committee and I disagree, we try to reach an agreement. But my neck is on the line. Teachers have tenure; I don't."

Catherine listened to Samantha intently. "Have you ever taken the time to consider why some things are done the way they are done? In other words, could budgets be apportioned differently? What should be the role of teachers and administrators in observing and evaluating? Could there be other critical committees, and if so, could the final authority be configured differently? Who does the hiring and firing?"

"Now wait a minute, Catherine! We have collective bargaining agreements that clearly stipulate that it is the responsibility of the administration to evaluate, and we have policies about budgets. And what about your job? You have staffers who work for you. They don't vote on every issue. You hire them, evaluate them, and even may have to fire them. There is an expectation that you're the boss. Each of you has specific tasks and responsibilities. So while you work in a democratic government, your daily life is not democratic."

"You're absolutely right, Samantha. I'm not talking, though, about voting on everything. I'm not talking about you giving up your power and authority. However, I am asking you to reconsider how power and responsibility are configured. Maybe your leadership team should reexamine some of the principles that our democratic country was founded on. Maybe some of those democratic attributes could lead you in a new way of thinking."

Samantha looked quite skeptical. "What principles are you talking about? Specifically?"

Catherine walked to her small desk that sat in front of the window overlooking the street below. She pulled out a collection of documents and returned to sit down with Samantha. Over the next two hours they read, debated, laughed, and argued.

KEY POINTS

- Bureaucracies perform necessary functions, but they are designed to maintain the status quo, not lead to change.
- Critical Theory can provide a lens through which we examine our school power and authority structures.
- Open Systems thinking and the newer sciences provide a more natural model for school systems than Closed Systems thinking and the Newtonian sciences.
- While school leaders would have us believe our systems are tightly controlled, the reality is they are loosely coupled. Yet administrators and politicians strive for more control in their policies and mandates.

POINTS TO PONDER

1. What parts of your school bureaucracy do you need to keep? Why?
2. What parts of your school do you need to examine through a critical lens?
3. What are the "three discourse values" necessary for you to ensure democratic dialogue?
4. How is Open Systems thinking different than Closed Systems thinking? What remnants of closed models does your school still use?
5. What are some practical lessons from the newer sciences?
6. What are some lessons from loosely coupled systems?

NOTES

1. Wayne Hoy and Cecil Miskel, *Educational Administration: Theory, Research, and Practice* (New York: Random House, 1982).
2. For a more detailed description of Professional Bureaucracies, the reader is invited to read Henry Minzberg, *The Structuring of Organizations* (Englewood Cliffs, NJ: Prentice-Hall, 1979).
3. Francis X. Neumann Jr., "Organizational Structures to Match the New Information Rich Environments: Lessons from the Study of Chaos," *Public Productivity and Management Review* 21(1) (September 1997): 89.
4. L. Rhodes, "Connecting Leadership and Learning," *The American Association of School Administrators National Center for Connected Learning* (April 1997): 16.
5. William E. Halal, *The New Management: Bringing Democracy and Markets Inside Organizations* (San Francisco: Berrett Koehler, 1998).
6. Ibid., Rhodes, 43.
7. Charles Heckscher, "Defining the Post-Bureaucratic Type," in Charles Heckscher and Anne Donnellon, eds., *The Post-Bureaucratic Organization: New Perspectives on Organizational Change* (Thousand Oaks, CA: Sage, 1994).
8. Harvie Ramsay, "Industrial Democracy and the Question of Control," in E. Davis and Russell Lansbury, *Democracy and Control in the Workplace* (Melbourne, Australia: Longman Cheshire, 1986).
9. Ibid., Heckscher, 20–21.

10. Patrick Dolan, *Restructuring Our Schools: A Primer on Systemic Change* (Kansas City, MO: Systems and Organizations, 1994), 34 and 30. This book is a foundational book to understand how school systems are currently structured and why, and how people can begin to make some fundamental changes—with real-life applications.

11. Ibid., Rhodes, 17.

12. Ibid., Heckscher, 24.

13. D. Dotlich and P. Cairo, *Unnatural Leadership: Going Against Intuition and Experience to Develop Ten New Leadership Instincts* (San Francisco: Jossey-Bass, 2002).

14. This quote was cited in Howard Zinn, *Declarations of Independence: Cross-Examining American Ideology* (New York: Harper Collins, 1990), 6. Zinn referenced J. le Carré's *The Russian House* (Knopf, 1989), 207. Zinn goes on to express the radical nature of Critical Theory. In his words (page 2), "If those in charge of our society—politicians, corporate executives, and owners of press and television—can dominate our ideas, they will be secure in their power. They will not need soldiers patrolling the streets. We will control ourselves."

15. Russ Marion, *Leadership in Education: Organizational Theory for the Practitioner* (Upper Saddle River, NJ: Merrill Prentice Hall, 2002), 252. For an excellent synopsis of Critical Theory the reader is invited to read the work of Viviane Robinson, "Critical Theory and the Social Psychology of Change," in K. Leithwood et al., eds., *International Handbook of Educational Leadership and Administration* (Amsterdam: Kluwer Academic Publishers, 1996), 1069–96.

16. L. Beyer, "The Value of Critical Perspectives in Teacher Education," *Journal of Teacher Education* 52(2) (March/April 2001): 151–63.

An excellent critique of Critical Theory is provided by Maxim Voronov and Peter T. Coleman of Columbia University. In their article, "Beyond the Ivory Towers: Organizational Power Practices and a 'Practical' Critical Postmodernism," *The Journal of Applied Behavioral Science* 39(2) (June 2003): 169–85, they state, "Primary power defines the domain. A manager is able to give orders and to expect them to be followed because their role of a manager has been historically constructed so as to include notions of order giving. It is important to recognize that the various sources of power are not concrete but socially constructed" (174). Similarly, "Critical Theory deals with power and is aimed at emancipation," Fritjof Capra, *The Hidden Connections: A Science of Sustainable Living* (New York: Anchor Books, 2004), 79. Howard Zinn, *Declarations of Independence: Cross-Examining American Ideology* (New York: Harper Perennial, 1990), 5, further stipulates, "What normally operates the day by day is the quiet dominance of certain ideas, the ideas we are expected to hold by our neighbors, our employers, and our political leaders; the ones we quickly learn are the most acceptable. The result is an obedient, acquiescent, passive citizenry—a situation that is deadly to democracy."

17. Ibid., Zinn, 219.

18. J. Jermier, "Critical Perspectives on Organizational Control," *Administrative Science Quarterly* 43 (1998): 235. Jermier explained how this control has moved from a more transparent form to a more menacing one:

> Managerial practices moved away from widespread reliance on coercive control in the late-nineteenth century toward technological control (such as assembly line) and then, by the mid-twentieth century, to bureaucratic forms of control (246).

The reader is asked to consider how contemporary organizations allow administrators to read and monitor employees' e-mail, and in some cases hidden cameras are used. Jermier then explained even further, more subtle, forms of control and manipulation with

> how MBO's [Management by Objectives] requirements for documenting performance augmented the disciplinary power of senior partners by enhancing their surveillance over junior partners. Mentoring, in turn, softened MBO's disciplinary power by encouraging junior partners to confess their failings and other inner truths. Their mentors could then legitimately exercise pastoral power by counseling their juniors on how to bring their behavior into line with the firm's expectations. The result was that junior partners became accomplices in transforming themselves from autonomous professionals into "corporate clones" (247–48).

19. Maxim Voronov and Peter T. Coleman, "Beyond the Ivory Towers: Organizational Power Practices and a 'Practical' Critical Postmodernism," *The Journal of Applied Behavioral Sciences* 39(2) (June 2003): 172.

> For example, critical theorists have asserted that the quality of life, worker satisfaction, and participative management concerns expressed by human relations scholars are little more than clever ways to quell any potential for employee resistance and to increase managerial control over organizations. They argue, for example, that feeling empowered is not the same thing as being empowered. Choosing one of the limited options for getting the work done, in which both the agenda and the methods are defined by the management, is not empowering. Whereas more traditional management scholars take the managerial point of view, critical theorists take the employee perspective. The goal of critical theorists is to expose systems of domination and to reform organizations to create new organizational arrangements, which would be free of exploitative power arrangements and distorted communication.

Voronov and Coleman continue, "Those in the lower echelons of the hierarchy often are 'duped' by those at the top into believing that they are empowered, although in reality they are still being controlled from above and by each other through ideology or disciplinary power" (176).

20. Ibid., 173.

21. Perry Rettig, "Beyond Organizational Tinkering: A New View of School Reform," in *Educational Horizons* 48(4) (Summer 2004): 264.

22. For a most insightful examination of Critical Theory's application to the educational enterprise, the reader is invited to read Paulo Freire's *Pedagogy of the Oppressed* (New York: Continuum, 1970).

23. In a most eloquent fashion, Comstock wrote:

Beginning from the practical problems of everyday existence it [critical dialogue] returns to that life with the aim of enlightening its subjects about unrecognized social constraints and possible courses of action by which they may liberate themselves. Its aim is enlightened self-knowledge and effective political action. Its method is dialogue, and its effect is to heighten its subjects' self-awareness of their collective potential as the active agents of history.

D. Comstock, "A Method for Critical Research," in E. Bredo and W. Feinberg, eds., *Knowledge and Values in Social and Educational Research* (Philadelphia: Temple University Press, 1982), 382. Cited in Viviane Robinson, "Critical Theory and the Social Psychology of Change," in K. Leithwood et al., eds., *International Handbook of Educational Leadership and Administration* (1996), 1070–71.

24. Viviane Robinson, "Critical Theory and the Social Psychology of Change," in Keith Leithwood et al., eds., *International Handbook of Educational Leadership and Administration,* (The Netherlands: Kluwer Academic Publishers, 1996): 1085–86.

25. Paulo Freire, *Pedagogy of the Oppressed* (New York: Continuum, 1970), 73. In a concurring opinion, Sirotnik explained, "In summarizing empirical research on 'the modal classroom,' . . . We are implicitly teaching dependence upon authority, linear thinking, social apathy, passive involvement, and 'hands-off learning,' all in a 'virtually affectless environment'" (Sirotnik, 1983, 29—cited in L. Beyer, "The Value of Critical Perspectives in Teacher Education," *Journal of Teacher Education* 52[2] [March/April 2001]: 155).

26. J. Bransford, A. Brown, and A. Cocking, eds., *How People Learn: Brain, Mind, Experience, and School* (Washington, DC: National Academy Press, 1999), 120.

27. Perry Rettig, *Quantum Leaps in School Leadership* (Lanham, MD: Rowman & Littlefield, 2002), 100.

28. Ibid., Beyer, 161.

29. William Bigelow, "Inside the Classroom: Social Vision and Critical Pedagogy," in *Teachers College Record* 91(3) (Columbia University: Teachers College, Spring 1990): 439, 445.

30. Fritjof Capra, *The Hidden Connections: A Science for Sustainable Living* (New York: Anchor Books, 2004), 75.

31. For an excellent review of Open Systems Theory and its derivatives, the reader is invited to read Russ Marion's *Leadership in Education: Organizational Theory for the Practitioner* (Upper Saddle River, NJ: Merrill Prentice Hall, 2002).

32. John H. Clarke, "Growing High School Reform: Planting the Seeds of Systemic Change," *NASSP Bulletin* (April 1999): 1. Clarke explained his position: "Most of the energy for change, we believe, comes from those who are closest to the ground, teachers and students in classrooms. Most of the drive toward order, on the other hand, comes from central structures, district offices, and state agencies developing policies and procedures to keep the school running" (2–3).

33. Henry Stapp, *Mind, Matter, and Quantum Mechanics* (New York: Springer-Verlag, 1993), 14. In my earlier book, I spent a great deal of time covering these newer sciences, including quantum physics and its sundry experiments and theories, chaos theory, the science of complexity, ecology, dissipative structures, forces, and fields. These are all covered in easy-to-read lay descriptions—no math. These portrayals are followed with lengthier sections on implications and applications for school practitioners. Perry Rettig, *Quantum Leaps in School Leadership* (Lanham, MD: Rowman & Littlefield, 2002).

34. Victor Mansfield and J. Marvin Spiegelman, "On the Physics and Psychology of the Transference as an Interactive Field," *Journal of Analytical Psychology* 41 (1996): 193.

35. Joseph Jaworski, *Synchronicity: The Inner Path of Leadership* (San Francisco: Berrett-Koehler, 1996), 79.

36. Margaret Wheatley, *Leadership and the New Science*. Videorecording and Instructor's Manual (Carlsbad, CA: CRM Films, 1993).

37. Fritjof Capra, *The Web of Life: A New Scientific Understanding of Living Systems* (New York: Anchor Books Doubleday,1996), 190. Capra provides some wonderful insights into how human organizations are like natural systems. His depiction of our systems and their similarities to cells is most fascinating. "A cellular network is a nonlinear pattern of organization, and we need complexity theory (nonlinear dynamics) to understand its intricacies" (8). He went on to say:

Membranes are not only a universal characteristic of life, but also display the same type of structure throughout the living world. . . . A membrane is very different from a cell wall. Whereas cell walls are rigid structures, membranes are always active, opening and closing continually, keeping certain substances out and letting others in, and the membrane, by being semipermeable, controls their proportions and keeps them in balance. . . . Indeed, the first thing a bacterium does when it is attacked by another organism is to make membranes. . . . The cell does not contain several distinct membranes, but rather has one single, interconnected membrane system. This so-called "endomembrane system" is always in motion, wrapping itself around all the organelles and going out to the edge of the cell. It is a moving "conveyor belt" that is continually produced, broken down and produced again (8).

Finally, with regard to how these cells make up networks,

[t]he function of each component in this network is to transform or replace other components, so that the entire network continually generates itself. This is the key to the systemic definition of life: living networks continually create, or re-create, themselves by transforming or replacing their components. In this way they undergo continual structural changes while preserving their weblike patterns of organization (10).

38. Ibid., Wheatley, 78.
39. H. Gelatt, "Chaos and Compassion," in *Counseling and Values* 39(2) (January 1995): 108–16.
40. Ilya Prigogine and Irene Stengers, *Order Out of Chaos* (New York: Bantam Books, 1984), 14.
41. Jean Lipman-Blumen, *The Connective Edge: Leading in an Interdependent World* (San Francisco: Jossey-Bass, 1996), 78.
42. J. Kotter, *What Leaders Really Do* (Cambridge, MA: Harvard Business School Press, 1999), 4.
43. Ibid., Mansfield and Spiegelman, 192.
44. Throughout this chapter I have used the phrase "apparent chaos." That is because often what we *see* as organizational chaos may not *be* chaos. In a most erudite fashion, Paulson stated, "In the absence of an operational explanation of the passage between levels, observers experience the system's complexity as disorder or noise and must often negotiate with this presence of apparent randomness in constructing explanations." W. Paulson, "Literature, Complexity, Interdisciplinarity," in K. Hayles, ed., *Chaos and Order: Complex Dynamics in Literature and Science* (Chicago: University of Chicago Press, 1991), 46. Editor Hayles further stipulated, "Chaos remains the necessary other, the opaque turbulence—that challenges and complements the transparency of order. . . . In chaos theory chaos may either lead to order, as

it does with self-organizing systems, or in yin/yang fashion it may have deep structures of order encoded within it." Ibid., Hayles, 3.

45. Ibid., Capra, *The Hidden Connections*, 81, shows us that indeed natural sciences are models for human organizations. "The network is one of the very basic patterns of organization in all living systems. . . . Extending the systemic understanding of life to the social domain, therefore, means applying our knowledge of life's basic patterns and principles of organization, and specifically our understanding of living networks, to social reality."

46. In a most fascinating article, John H. Clarke, "Growing High School Reform: Planting the Seeds of Systemic Change," in *NASSP Bulletin* (April 1999), pages 4, 8, and 9, explained how he researched several high schools through a lens of the new sciences. "To understand how school reform occurs, one must look at the whole structure at once." By viewing the organization through a system's lens, Clarke noted,

> [o]ur study suggests that cross-boundary interaction is essential to systemic change in a high school. We found that system change becomes possible when individuals with different roles—students, teachers, school administrators, and policymakers—interact around a shared concern for student learning. . . . When communication stops, innovation also stops, starved of the energy required for growth. From the perspective we developed in this study, we began to doubt that systemic change can be planned, designed, or implemented using the mechanics of systems management. Seeing the components of a school as separate entities simply reinforces the sense of isolation experienced by the people who learn and teach daily within their separate cells. . . . High schools grow toward reform when all the parts interact constantly, forming an organism flexible enough to adapt to the pace of change in the surrounding environment.

47. James G. March and Johan P. Olsen, *Democratic Governance* (New York: The Free Press, 1995), 200 and 207, explained, "Effective variation and experimentation in governance involve 1) a willingness to take risks and 2) a willingness and capability to persist in a course of action despite early adverse signals." They further stipulated, "A political institution needs the *capability to experiment*. . . Some standard features of political democracy reduce capabilities of experimentation, particularly rules enforcing jurisdiction, standardization, and accountability."

48. Ibid., Neumann Jr., 95. In a similar vein, John H. Clarke, ibid., pages 2 and 4, explained, "Schools cannot improve student learning in a dormant state. . . . In complexity theory, change does not occur in a neat linear sequence, as mechanical systems often do. Instead, change occurs as a whole organism or physical structure responds to complex changes in its environment. . . . While they appear contradictory, energy and order are complementary impulses in the process of organic growth."

49. Ibid., Halal, 83.
50. Ibid., Rhodes, 15.
51. Ibid., Rhodes, 15.
52. Edward Greenberg, *Workplace Democracy: The Political Effects of Participation* (Ithaca, NY: Cornell University Press, 1986), 43.
53. Teresa Harrison, "Designing the Post-Bureaucratic Organization: New Perspectives on Organizational Change," *Australian Journal of Communication* 19, Brisbane, Australia (1992): 16–17.
54. Ibid., Harrison, 20, cited the work of DeWitt's review of the literature on employee responses to work, documents widespread demoralization of American industrial workers, and attributes this to the rigid hierarchical structure of modern organizations. S. DeWitt, *Worker Participation and the Crisis of Liberal Democracy* (Boulder, CO: Westview Press, 1980).
55. Ibid., Halal, 43. Other authors have cited similar concerns. From Fritjof Capra, *The Hidden Connections: A Science for Sustainable Living* (New York: Anchor Books, 2004), 105: "There is no room for flexible adaptations, learning, and evolution in the machine metaphor, and it is clear that organizations managed in strictly mechanistic ways cannot survive in today's complex, knowledge-oriented and rapidly changing business environment." Capra also suggests, "To run properly, a machine must be controlled by its operators, so that it will function according to their instructions. Accordingly, the whole thrust of classical management theory is to achieve efficient operations through top-down control. Living beings, on the other hand, act autonomously. They can never be controlled like machines. To try and do so is to deprive them of their aliveness" (104). From Robert Owens, *Organizational Behavior in Education: Adaptive Leadership and School Reform* (New York: Pearson Allyn & Bacon, 2004), 154: "Moreover, we understand now much better than we did twenty years ago that schools, like all organizations, are complex and confusing places that are—at their best—filled with contradictions, ambivalence, ambiguity, and uncertainty. These understandings help us realize that many of the most important problems confronting school administrators are neither clear-cut nor amenable to technical solutions." And from noted scientist Karl Weick, "Educational Organizations in Loosely Coupled Systems," *Administrative Science Quarterly* 21 (March 1976): 1: "[People believe that] an organization does what it does because of plans, intentional selection of means that get the organization to agree upon goals, and all of this is accomplished by such rationalized procedures as cost-benefit analysis, division of labor, specified areas of discretion, authority invested in the office, job descriptions, and a consistent evaluation and reward system. The only problem with that portrait is that it is rare in nature. People in organizations [rarely find this]."

56. Nitin Nohria and James D. Berkley, "The Virtual Organization: Bureaucracy, Technology, and the Implosion of Control," in Charles Heckscher and Lynda Applegate, eds., *The Post-Bureaucratic Organization: New Perspectives on Organizational Change* (Thousand Oaks, CA: 1994), 112.

57. Ibid., Harrison, 21.

58. Hilary Wainwright, *Reclaim the State: Experiments in Popular Democracy* (London: Verso, 2003), 25.

59. George Cheney et al., "Democracy, Participation, and Communication at Work: A Multidisciplinary Review," *Communication Yearbook* 21 (2004): 69.

60. Anne Donnellon and Maureen Scully, "Teams, Performance, and Rewards: Will the Post-Bureaucratic Organization be a Post-Meritocratic Organization?" in ibid., Heckscher and Applegate, 64.

61. Ibid., William E. Halal, xviii. Further, ibid., Nohria and Berkley, 117, cite the work of Frank Webster and Kevin Robins: "Taylor's goal was to isolate the 'brain' of the organization from the producing 'body' to create a management sector that could serve as a repository and processor of expropriated knowledge."

62. Ibid., March and Olsen, 193.

63. Fareed Zakaria, *The Future of Freedom: Illiberal Democracy at Home and Abroad* (New York: W. W. Norton & Company, 2003), 105.

CHAPTER 3

Democratic Principles: Change Happens

This book is about change. It's about changing organizational structures and administrative practices and even culture in order to be more congruous with the democratic principles by which we as a country feel so emboldened—yet principles that we leave at the front door of our workplaces.

But this book is more about changing our perceptions of what it means to be a professional within our organizations. It's about challenging our assumptions and maybe even giving us new lenses through which to look at our workplaces. By examining these foundational democratic principles through the lenses of Critical Theory and of the new sciences, we may create new ways of operating our professional bureaucracies, not because it will get more work out of our employees, but because it's the way we believe they should be treated.

We have come to assume that our institutions must have rigid, static structures—our mimetic isomorphism. However, if we go back to the sciences we learn that natural systems have fluid structures that respond to the environment. "The defining characteristic of an autopoietic system is that it undergoes continual structural changes while preserving its weblike pattern of organization."[1]

These dynamic structures allow for the system to respond to the ever-changing demands of the environment—to survive. Yet we spend a great deal of money, energy, and time attempting to maintain equilibrium, and we don't even realize we're killing our organizations.

Just how do these postmodern, natural concepts relate to our current, yet antiquated, organizations? According to Charles Heckscher:

> Bureaucracies tend to evolve not smoothly, but in fits and starts: Periods of routine are punctuated by intense periods of revolution from above. This results, again, primarily from the segmented structure: By design, only the top of the organization has a full picture of the whole plan of change. Those lower down see only the pieces that they are "assigned;" they are unable to adapt smoothly to the inevitable shifts in relations to other parts of the organization and have to refer problems for formal resolution to their bosses. This results in a tremendous grinding of the gears.[2]

Heckscher clearly elucidates the current affairs of our organizations, but then he gives us a glimpse of how we can begin to change our organizations in this postmodern world:

> There is a growing sense that effective organization change has its own dynamic, a process that cannot simply follow strategic shifts and that is longer and subtler than can be managed by any single leader. It is generated from the insights of many people trying to improve the whole, and it accumulates, as it were, over long periods. Dramatic moments of "revolutionary" transformation are only a small piece of it, and often are the most effective way to bring about change. If this is true—and there is much reason to believe it is—the bureaucratic structures are not the most effective ones for managing the process.[3]

We've been told that change is inevitable, but clearly people often face change with hesitation and opprobrium. According to Wells and Picou, "Innovations interrupt and change the status structure, and, as a result, the members of a changing organization may perceive a threat to their status security. In fact, 'status rewards' are sometimes redistributed and the real (or anticipated) loss of these rewards are grounds for threatened members to become resistors of change."[4]

In a concurring opinion, and related to Open Systems thinking, Heckscher, Eisenstat, and Rice stated, "When people agree to enter a dialogue, they know that the power relations will change—and they are not sure how. This is an example of 'bootstrapping'. . . . They cannot see the advantages of a higher-order system until they have entered it, but they fear it until they have understood it."[5] Democratic organizations will threaten these leaders.

Educators might have become victims of their own success and fearful of the requisite change. While it has taken decades for it to happen, teachers now get paid decent salaries, and their fringe benefits packages are quite good. They now have too much to lose. If they "rock the boat" or instigate change, their jobs or advancement opportunities may be put in jeopardy. When you don't have much, it's not such a big issue to risk it all. When you are comfortable, you risk a great deal by pushing the system to its bifurcation point.

Thus, people are afraid to begin the change process because they are afraid they may very well lose the position of their status (with associated pay and benefits), and they have no idea what they might end up doing when they come through the other end of the change process. Again, relating change to chaos theory—the process of change is related to the bifurcation point. When a natural system enters this stage, it can either leap to a higher order of complexity, or it can die—and that is the fear.

Management of the change process is designed to be very clean and precise in our modern organizations. In the words of Capra, "The principles of classical management theory have become so deeply ingrained in the ways we think about organizations that for most managers the design of formal structures, linked by clear lines of communication, coordination, and control, has become almost second nature. We shall see that this largely unconscious embrace of the mechanistic approach to management is one of the main obstacles to organizational change today."[6]

This traditional model for directing change is invariably instigated from on top—by design. As posited by Wells and Picou, "Innovation tends to be structured either directly or indirectly by people, especially administrators, who are in the necessary power positions to bring about changes."[7] This top-down approach to creating change is often not embraced by the workers.

Without employee support, however, full implementation is not likely. Again, Wells and Picou: "It seems then, that some sort of antagonistic cooperation between faculty and administration is a necessary condition for successful educational innovation."[8] This antagonism is the practical flaw in classical methods of creating change.

Heckscher, Eisenstat, and Rice have explicated three typical approaches managers use to try to control change:

1. They could restructure by command: move managers around, reduce layers, promote those with skills and values that are seen by the top as needed, push authority down for operational decisions in the organization, change job descriptions and rewards—in general, clean up and reconfigure the organization to meet what the top sees as the new problem.
2. They could focus on an attempt to create a shared commitment to the change through forceful communication from the top, explaining the rationale and strategy—using anything from videotapes to extensive workshops at all levels.
3. They could try to develop the change in a more opportunistic way, without making grand statements to the organization about what is going on. The leaders could seek to build coalition for change through their individual interactions with organizational "champions," hoping that a gradual accumulation of new approaches would add up to a transformation.

"The first of these choices," believe Heckscher, Eisenstat, and Rice, "is an example of the use of traditional bureaucratic command."[9] This option is clearly accomplished through top-down autocratic processes. The second two options are more versions of Human Relations Approaches of apparent employee empowerment, still, however, under the direction of administration.

Modern, industrial approaches to the change process followed lessons from the sciences of Closed Systems thinking. These models understood change to happen in slow, equilibrial steps.[10] The notion believes change is linear and can be clearly planned and replicated. These models look good when put on paper, but they are fundamentally flawed in practice. Yet our organizations are not doomed to this morose pattern.

New dynamic models of change, congruent with natural Open Systems thinking, are beginning to emerge for our postmodern world. Punctuated equilibrium is perhaps the most terrifying to people. In nature, we find examples where floods, hurricanes, tornadoes, wildfire, and other natural disasters wipe out the current ecosystem. Yet new life emerges.

March and Olsen explain how punctuated equilibrium sneaks up on organizations. "The old institutional order collapses, and a new order is created. . . . Once created, an institution usually becomes relatively stable, its initial character being sustained by internal dynamics that resist change even though environmental conditions continue to evolve.

"Changes in the environment are likely to be ignored, fought, or buffered if they can be. Core practices and beliefs are likely to be defended rather than made consistent with new environmental pressures."[11] In other words, our system culture makes every attempt to maintain the status quo.

Earlier, we learned from Francis Neumann Jr. that modern organizations assume that their systems operate in an environment of equilibrium. However, Neumann—citing Kiel—explained that postmodern organizations live in a different environment:

> [Kiel] suggested that nonequilibrium processes appear to be more descriptive of the interactions of *democratic* [emphasis added] societies, in which the political process brings external energy into the system and drives it far from stability. It is the nonlinear process that allows the system to incorporate change within itself and to adapt to changing external environments. Kiel also suggested that agents can purposefully force change in organizations toward the points of chaotic thresholds.[12]

Thus, while administrative leaders may not be able to control system change, comprehensive administrative reform is a most plausible strategy for "democratic institutional adaptation."[13] Again, earlier in this chapter, Heckscher, Eisenstat, and Rice showed us three Closed Systems approaches to working with change. They have also postulated a fourth Open Systems approach.

In this fourth type,

> [leaders] could initiate an open and public process of self-examination without closely predefining the solution, aimed at developing a deeper understanding of the organization's capabilities and the challenges it faces—with the hope that a shared strategy would emerge from the process. . . . *Only the fourth type—collaborative change—establishes*

the conditions for a successful transition to a post-bureaucratic model [italics in original]. It is, in effect, the change process that "matches" the new form of organization. The others may create enthusiasm and a sense of change for a time, but they fail to break through the boundaries that define the essentially bureaucratic paradigm—thereby ending up at best as types of "successful failures."[14]

Postmodern leadership approaches require looking at the change process through new lenses. By looking through these lenses, we learn some new lessons:

- "Change usually comes in the manner of a corkscrew rather than a hammer."[15]
- Change takes time and persistence.
- Individuals go through stages in the change process and have different needs at different stages.
- Change strategies are most effective when they are chosen to meet people's needs.
- Administrative support and approval is needed for change to occur.
- Developing a critical mass of support is just as important as developing administrative support.
- An individual or committee must take responsibility for organizing and managing the change.[16]

Mundry and Hergert cited the Concerns Based Adoption Model (CBAM) to organizational change as developed by Loucks and Hall. They described four additional points:

1. Change is a process, not an event.
2. The individual needs to be the primary focus of intervention for change in the organization.
3. Change is a highly personal experience.
4. Individuals experience developmental growth in feelings and skills.[17]

Finally, in the research they collected in developing their *Change Game*, Mundry and Hergert explained the kinds of support needed to make change occur:

- The approval of the administration is crucial to the success of making change. There must be backing from a key administrator in order to initiate the change process.
- A broad base of support from the school and its community is necessary to implement the innovation.
- It is necessary to provide training and assistance even after the program is underway.
- To sustain an innovation, people must pay attention to institutionalizing it.[18]

A couple of common threads are found in this research. Change is about people more than it is about structure. Both leaders and workers must be supportive of the change, and it takes time and process to be sustained. The complex nature of contemporary organizations and of the highly skilled work environment necessitates this group involvement. Donnellon and Scully noted:

> As organizations adopt both efficiency and effectiveness as strategic goals, many of their critical tasks . . . now require knowledge and experience that do not reside in one person but are distributed among people, making them interdependent. Furthermore, this interdependence takes on the reciprocal quality that renders the tasks impossible to accomplish except by a group or team. Thus, the predictable synergistic outcomes that may arise when members from different parts of the organization get together to work on a problem have become more of a necessity than a luxury and teams are the common solution.[19]

It is the contention of this book that in order for our school systems to survive and flourish, fundamental organizational changes must occur. Through the lens of Critical Theory, we should reexamine our founding democratic principles for direction. Yet our contemporary operating procedures are far from democratic, and we ourselves will most likely fight this change.

March and Olsen noted, "The development of bureaucratic expertise, position, and isolation becomes an oligarchic threat to democracy."[20] So before we begin an analysis of our founding principles, let us examine concerns of democratic governance.

Not only are there perceived hurdles in the school setting, but even the private sector shares these obstacles to reform. In his study of cooperative enterprises in the United States, Edward Greenberg highlighted this concern:

> The paradox of enterprise authoritarianism operating within a formally democratic political system is particularly marked in the United States, where surprisingly few advances have been made toward democracy in the workplace and the distribution and practice of formal democratic rights and liberties are theoretically the most wide-spread. As a condition of earning a living, American workers must give up their accustomed rights and privileges of citizenship upon crossing the threshold of the factory gate or office door. Within the business firm, the rights of free speech, free association, election of leadership, and general control of collective policy—so central to most definitions of the democratic polity—are not generally considered to be in effect.[21]

Even more, administrators and employees alike have grave concerns about making our work organizations democratic. Change in power structures is invariably a concern when it comes to empowering employees. Managers may feel that they will lose their prestige and even their jobs—that they will no longer be needed in these postmodern organizations.[22]

Management will claim that as they move into democratic organizations, they retain all their former responsibility yet lose their previous autonomy[23] and power.[24] Allowing for fuller employee participation could even cause employees to begin to question management's legitimacy to claim authority.[25]

Workers and staff can also see concerns about perceived shifts in power; they may well believe that management's move to empowering employees is disingenuous. In other words, they have experienced the manipulation of Human Relations Approaches to employee empowerment. In fact, it has been noted earlier that moves to apparent democratization of the workplace may indeed be manipulation by administration to gain even more control.

According to John Smyth, "The basic argument is that moves towards devolution, in most cases, are not fundamentally about grassroots democratic reform of education aimed at giving schools and their communities more power—rather, they are about precisely the reverse, namely, the intensification of central control, while seeming to be otherwise."[26]

This Critical Theory perspective of insidious manipulation views management's "giving away power" as their way to get employees to do what management wants, but letting workers believe they are empowered when they truly are not. In regard to how employees are permitted to speak freely, most often their freedom is limited.

Noted historian Howard Zinn explained, "The problem with free speech in the United States is not with the *fact* [emphasis in original] of access, but with the degree of it. There is *some* access to dissident views, but these are pushed to the corner."[27]

A very legitimate concern with new democratic structures is that, because that's all they know, the oppressed will become the oppressors.[28] As pointed out by postmodernists, institutionalizing a new order might simply lead to new power arrangements and produce new inequalities. "Postmodernism is suspicious of all grand narratives and points out the potential for domination inherent even in the best of intentions," according to Voronov and Coleman.[29]

In a concurring opinion, Fareed Zakaria exclaimed, "The tendency for a democratic government to believe it has absolute sovereignty (that is, power) can result in the centralization of authority, often by extraconstitutional means and with grim results."[30] Hence the maxim: "Power corrupts and absolute power corrupts absolutely."

Besides issues related to power, employers and employees alike have other concerns about democratic models. First and foremost, people are afraid of an organizational bifurcation where the system will either leap into a higher complexity—democratization of the workplace—or fall into chaos and die. Again, in the words of Voronov and Coleman, "Emancipation may result in a profound confusion, general distrust, and depression.[31]

Chaos can lead to another fear—the fear of vice. "Corruption thrives on disorganization, the absence of stable relationships among groups and of recognized patterns of authority.[32] Still, chaos theory may be a perfect model for us to conceptualize how we deal with change in our organizations.[33] "Difficulties arise primarily from the unstable dynamics of multigroup solidarity. Solidarity thrives on conflict among groups," stated March and Olsen.[34]

In a most erudite insight, Bachrach and Botwinick explained, "The idea of democracy can continue to function as a creatively disruptive force in the polity, especially in provoking protest and struggle against the contradiction between oligarchical rule in the workplace and the idea of democracy."[35]

Pragmatic concerns also swirl around democratization of the workplace. It has been expressed that democracies are inefficient.[36] From concerns of inefficiency, people also worry that democratic decision making takes too much time. John Smyth explained, "A great deal of time of teachers can be diverted away from the primary task of teaching and learning. The energies of the principal can also be diverted away from being the educational leader."[37]

This may result in workers becoming full-time democratic representatives.[38] Gamson and Levin cite "four problems in democratic decision making that appear frequently enough to constitute common issues." These are:

1. The legitimate exercise of authority;
2. obtaining accountability from members;
3. the productive use of conflict; and
4. the productive use of meetings.[39]

Indeed, there are numerous concerns as we look to move toward more democratic organizations. These concerns could be enumerated as follows:

- *Appearance of democracy*: Are these changes real, or are they a disingenuous manipulation by leadership to keep workers and parents in line?
- *Degree of democracy*: Associated with the first concern is the question about how much voice will be given to the workers and families? In what areas will they be able to participate?
- *Power structures*: Will old power structures simply be replaced by new power structures? Will management lose power? Will new forms of oppression be created?
- *Accountability and representation*: Who will be held accountable for decisions and results? Who is in charge? Will all groups be represented and given voice?

- *Efficiency*: How much time will this take? Will the process of democratic decision making be inefficient and unproductive?

Even if we are successful in fully implementing genuine participatory decision-making systems, we need to continually examine and audit these systems, processes, and structures. "Ultimately, each presumed case of workplace democratization needs careful scrutiny with respect to such dimensions as (a) the range of issues about which participants may speak, (b) the extent of actual influence by employees through their exercise of voice, and (c) the levels of the hierarchy at which meaningful voice is possible."[40] Chapters 4 and 5 will revisit these concerns and provide a vision of appropriate checks and balances.

DEMOCRATIC PRINCIPLES

"There is an unmistakable contradiction between the democratic values of freedom and independence and the colonial and patriarchal strategies used to manage our organizations."[41] Peter Block used these words to alert us to the incongruence between our country's democratic ideals and the everyday practices of our places of employment. But what precisely are the democratic values and principles that we hold so dear? Specifically, which values and principles can we relate directly to our places of employment, to our schools?

Can democratic principles even be applied to our work environments? Edward Greenberg is emphatic in this affirmation. "Complex, modern institutions can be successfully operated on a basis of democratic, egalitarian, and nonhierarchical principles even in an environment that is hostile to such principles in the workplace in the United States."[42]

Charles Heckscher explicated, *"The central theoretical claim of post-bureaucratic organizations is that it is possible to make binding decisions without relying on offices* [emphasis in original]. This claim in turn relies on two concepts unfamiliar to bureaucracy: consensual legitimation and process."[43] In other words, the people who will be impacted by the decision need to be brought together to establish a process for making the decision and then to share in the dialogue in making the decision.

Before we examine our country's founding documents, it is important that we consider a few of the core values that helped the framers put these seminal works together.[44] Five essential core values that we can relate to our workplaces are liberty, common good, justice, equality, and diversity. *Liberty* refers to personal freedom and "the right to a free flow of information and ideas, open debate and [the] right to assembly." For the workplace, the *common good* means that each worker is committed to work with their fellow employees for "the greater benefit of all."

For *justice* to exist, workers "should be treated fairly . . . in the gathering of information and making of decisions." *Equality* requires that "there should be no class hierarchy sanctioned by law" and inordinate economic inequality. Finally, in order to ensure *diversity*, we need a "variety in culture and ethnic background, race, lifestyle, and belief." (Some readers may feel that these fundamental constitutional values were taken out of context to be applied to the workplace. The reader is invited to read the full document as cited in the endnotes following this chapter.)

It would appear that these fundamental beliefs have as their core tenets the belief in honesty, openness, and fairness. Workers must be treated fairly, open communication and decision making are essential, and processes must be transparent.

According to Constitutioncenter.org, there are eight constitutional principles. These are Rule of Law, Separation of Powers, Representative Government, Checks and Balances, Individual Rights, Freedom of Religion, Federalism, and Civilian Control of the Military. The first four are most striking for the discussion at hand. For the *rule of law*, it would seem apparent that all members of an organization should be held to the same rules, regulations, and standards, and that they be treated fairly.

For the government, the *separation of powers* doctrine provides for the legislative, executive, and judicial branches so that these powers "should be exercised by different institutions in order to maintain the limitations placed upon them." The doctrine of the separation of powers is designed so that no one person or body has too much power.

In the words of noted historian Samuel Huntington, "The passion of the Founding Fathers for the division of power, for setting ambition against ambition, for creating a constitution with a complicated system of balances exceeding that of any other, is, of course, well known. Everything is bought at a price, however, and . . . one apparent price of the division of power is government inefficiency."[45] As our systems currently stand, one might consider that we do have some separation of powers.

At a district level, we have administration, board of education, and teacher unions. The balance of power between these three groups, however, is certainly not clear, nor is it balanced. At the school level, we have administration, various working committees, and perhaps a Site Council. A democratic model will be explicated in the next chapter—where we will set forth a structure for the balance of powers and a system of checks and balances. While Huntington mentioned democratic models are inefficient, our current hierarchical systems are no models of efficiency!

In the workplace, *representative government* starts with the premise that the workers represent themselves, either directly or indirectly, through elected representation. The critical point is that the workers are truly empowered. In the doctrine of *checks and balances,* "the powers given to the different branches of government should be balanced, that is roughly equal, so that no branch can completely dominate the others."

"Branches of government are also given powers to check the power of other branches." In school systems, it is quite obvious that the executive "branch" has an inordinate amount of power. And there exists no judicial branch. In a strikingly similar tone to that of Samuel Huntington, contemporary historian Fareed Zakaria states, "Constitutionalism, as it was understood by its greatest eighteenth-century exponents, such as Montesquieu and Madison, is a complicated system of checks and balances designed to prevent the accumulation of power and the abuse of office. . . . Various groups must be included and empowered because, as Madison explained, 'ambition must be made to counteract ambition.'"[46]

The reader can judge for their own particular circumstance to what degree their school balances or limits power and provides for a system of checks and balances. The dual doctrines of the separation of powers and of checks and balances are critical to rethinking the ways we structure our schools. So more time and detail will be spent with them in the next chapter.

It is time for us to now turn our attention to some of the details in the founding documents of our country for possible insights to this goal of creating democratic workplaces. In our nation's constitution, we find several articles and sections to be applicable to the workplace.

The first half of the second paragraph to the Declaration of Independence reads, "*We hold these truths to be self-evident, that all men are created equal, that they are endowed by their Creator with certain inalienable Rights, that among these are Life, Liberty, and the pursuit of Happiness. That to secure these rights, Governments are instituted among Men, deriving their just powers from the consent of the governed.*" There are at least two lessons we can take away from these introductory sentences.

First, we should, without question, understand that all individuals are created equal. While we may not have equal training, knowledge, skills, responsibilities, and the like, we should all be valued as equal. We could quibble that an important distinction is that the original document clearly states that "all men are *created* equal," and that because of our roles and responsibilities, we are no longer equal at work. The point is that each of us brings special value to our organizations and needs to be treated with dignity and respect.

Second, our institutions are developed and maintained by people, and the people who are designated with power and authority derive that power and authority from the employees or constituent groups. This latter point is crucial. Our leaders are given their authority, not by some impersonal legalistic or rational agreements, but directly from the workers and their communities.

Numerous lessons can be learned from the U.S. Constitution. In Article I, Section 1, we learn that *All legislative Powers herein granted shall be vested in a Congress of the United States, which shall consist of a Senate and a House of Representatives.* Sections 2 and 3 of Article I explicate how members of Congress—the House of Representatives and the Senate, respectively, will be apportioned and elected.

Appropriate details will be covered in the next chapter of this book. From Article I, Section 1, however, we may interpret that the workers (and even students and their families) are represented by people whom they choose.

The two types of representation—House of Representatives and Senate—allow for a balance of powers. In other words, it provides for both majority rule and protection of the rights of the minority. Section 4 states that "The Congress shall assemble at least once in every Year."

Section 5 stipulates, "Each House shall keep a Journal of its Proceedings, and from time to time publish the same." From these two sections we learn that our representative bodies need to meet to deal with the organization's business on at least an annual basis and that this business must be recorded for all to see; this will provide the requisite transparency to deliberations.

Section 6 speaks to compensation of representatives and that they are forbidden to concurrently hold two offices. Section 7 is reserved to discussion of procedures for bills to become laws. Here, we learn that bills must be passed by both houses of Congress and the president. If the president (Executive) vetoes a bill, it can be overturned by a two-thirds majority vote by the House.

Again, we can apply lessons from this section of the Constitution to our workplaces. In order to balance the power, representative committees can promote policies or resolutions, but they need a majority vote and approval from other constituents. For example, a school's Site Council may wish to put forth a particular resolution, but the resolution could be denied by the principal.

Article II of the U.S. Constitution speaks to the power of the Executive branch. Section 1, in particular, dictates that, "The executive Power shall be vested in a President of the United States of America." Section 3 further stipulates that "He shall from time to time give to the Congress Information of the State of the Union, and recommend to their Consideration such Measures as he shall judge necessary and expedient." In a school, we may consider the principal to be the executive who must report to the school's constituents as a matter of fact.

Article III of the U.S. Constitution is reserved for discussion of the Judicial branch. Section I begins with the following: "The judicial Power of the United States, shall be vested in one supreme Court, and in such inferior Courts as the Congress may from time to time ordain and establish."

This concept will be covered in much more depth in the next chapter; however, for now we can consider the importance of a third power to establish a firm rule of checks and balances and to hear grievances of the people. Further, the Judicial branch has the ability to declare any executive rule unconstitutional. While an individual school may not have a governing body serving in the role as an impartial judiciary, the school district may convene such a representative body.

The first three Articles of the U.S. Constitution are reserved for the three branches of the federal government. Article IV addresses issues related to how the various states interact and their rights. Article V speaks of amendments to the Constitution. Of particular interest is the first sentence in Section 1—"The Congress, whenever two thirds of both Houses shall deem it necessary, shall propose Amendments to the Constitution." Articles VI and VII refer to the authority of the new nation and ratification of the state constitutions.

The first ten amendments to the Constitution are known as the Bill of Rights. The First Amendment states, "Congress shall make no law respecting an establishment of religion, or prohibiting the free exercise thereof; or abridging the freedom of speech, or of the press; or the right of the people peaceably to assemble, and to petition the Government for a redress of grievances." When employees cross the doorway at work, they should not lose their rights of free speech and assembly. And they should be able to challenge management's decisions, all without fear of retribution.

Seventeen additional amendments to the Constitution followed the original Bill of Rights. The Twelfth Amendment states, "The Electors shall meet in their respective states and vote by ballot for President and Vice-President." Simply said, the people (workers and families) should vote for their executive. This is clearly a very controversial issue and will be covered in more detail in the subsequent chapter.

The Seventeenth Amendment modifies Article I, Section 3 of the U.S. Constitution by defining the term of Senators. The Twentieth Amendment further modifies Article I, Section 4 of the Constitution by defining the terms of the Executive branch and requirements of assembly of Congress. Limiting the president to two terms in office was the direction of the Twenty-Second Amendment. This amendment is mentioned here only because this author strongly does not believe that the school's executive officer should have term limits.

Now, what are the lessons we can take from these historical documents? From the Declaration of Independence we learn of the natural and inherent equality of the people and the need to treat everyone with dignity and respect. Furthermore, all governance power and authority is derived from the people.

From Article I of the Constitution, we learn of representative government, the need for balance of power, majority rule with the protection of rights of the minority, the need for regular public meetings of the representative bodies, the need for transparency to deliberations, the need for open records, that persons cannot serve on two governing bodies at once (principle of balance of power), and how rules and policies can be made (principle of checks and balances).

Article II of the U.S. Constitution tells us that the executive reports to the people. Article III shows us that a judicial body is needed for checks and balances and to allow for the people to air their grievances. Article V explains how amendments are to be made.

The Bill of Rights and the other amendments to the U.S. Constitution have two implications for schools. In the First Amendment, we learn that we must provide for freedom of speech and assembly, and we need to create a place and procedures for the workers to challenge their officials. The Twelfth Amendment explains that the people vote for their executive.

It would seem then, that democratic institutions are founded with the understanding of several key values and with a number of critical procedures, protocols, and doctrines in place in order to make these democratic values transpire. The critical attributes of any democratic institution, therefore, are:

- *Liberty*: personal freedom, free flow of information and ideas, open debate, and freedom of assembly.[47]
- *Common Good*: greater benefit for all; majority rule while protecting the rights of the minority.[48]
- *Justice*: fair treatment, shared decision making.[49]
- *Equality*: no class hierarchy.[50]
- *Diversity*: diversity and representation of both the people and of opinions.[51]
- *Honesty*, *Openness*, and *Fairness*: in all interactions with each other.[52]

In order for these values to become alive, certain mechanisms and institutional behaviors must take place. Decision making must be shared, transparent, and open.[53] This requires that information be shared freely with the people. The people need to be truly empowered. Where it is too cumbersome to be done directly, indirect empowerment must be created through representative government.

In order to guard against any one person or group from becoming dominant, a system of checks and balances needs to exist.[54] This leads to a separation of powers in order to limit the powers of any person or governing body.[55] Finally, a rule of law (or policies and rules) must be established to provide for fairness and equity.[56]

March and Olsen link the political ideas of democracy to our public institutions. "An institutionalized, free public sphere based on popular participation, public reasoning, criticism, and justification is supposed to guarantee truth-oriented opinion formation and the development of authentic identities.

"Public deliberation and majority voting institutionalized in representative assemblies are supposed to secure political equality in political decision making. Bureaucratically organized agencies are supposed to assure efficient, qualified, and impartial implementation of policies."[57] Hilary Wainwright promulgated several imperative conditions in order for democratic participation to exist:

> In order for participatory democracy to attain its own legitimacy . . . certain conditions need to be in place. First, if any form of participatory democracy is to achieve legitimacy as a source of power over decisions concerning the government of a locality, it needs to be open at its foundations to everyone affected by such decisions—even if only a minority participate. Openness is not just a formality. . . . Second, there need to be mutually agreed and openly negotiated rules. . . . A third condition, always difficult to preserve, is the autonomy of the participatory process from the state. . . . But these relationships depend on equality: participatory institutions need to have their own life and dynamism, and know that the elected body respects this. This egalitarianism leads to a fourth condition: the genuine sharing of knowledge. . . . The process must get results. It must not be seen as just another consultation exercise that leads nowhere.[58]

To which Cheney and his collaborators added, "Generally speaking, we characterize workplace democracy as referring to those principles and practices designed to engage and 'represent' (in the multiple senses of the term) as many relevant individuals and groups as possible in the formulation, execution, and modification of work-related activities."[59]

A variety of scholars in democratic workplaces have explicated these concepts, and it would be worthwhile to hear at least a portion of their reasoning. Liberty demands personal freedom, a free flow of information, open debate, and freedom of assembly. To this end, Cheney et al. further stipulate, "democratization can be operationally defined in terms of the extent of genuine opportunities for dissent and discussion."[60] We must ensure that teachers, students, and parents are not punished for sharing their concerns. In fact, we must provide opportunities for people to meet and discuss.

When it comes to supporting the common good, we find that decision making must be based upon an equitable voting system. From their review of the literature, March and Olsen added that there are "several fundamental rights and rules necessary for a democratic process: open inquiry, discussion, enlightened understanding, equal consideration, effective participation, and a decision reached by some system of voting that respects the essential equality of the citizens."[61]

Not only must people have a say in issues that impact them, but they must be able to vote where prudent. Further, all groups need to be represented, and their representatives must be chosen by the constituents.

Identification of democratic governing principles and values is critical as we begin to draw inferences to the workplace. Putting them into practice will be quite a task. Chapters 4 and 5 will develop implications for developing democratic schools and applications for the workplace.

Before we return to our journey with Principal Samantha Levy, let us learn from the personal perspective of an experienced and current board of education member who has participated in a tenuous and fruitful process of moving from a traditional governance structure to one of shared governance and decision making.

BOARD OF EDUCATION PERSPECTIVE

The Napoleon Area City School District (NACS) is a consolidated system of approximately two thousand students located in Northwest Ohio. It is fairly typical in demographics with many midsized districts in rural Midwestern America. Approximately half of the students are eligible for federal free or reduced lunch programs. Student academic performance has always been above the state average for Ohio and in the top half of peer school systems. It is largely a blue-collar and farming community.

The friction points in the district have been chiefly two: (1) up until approximately 2010 there had been roughly thirty years of turmoil and friction between the administration and the certificated staff. This culminated in a bitter strike in the mid '90s, which the community still has not forgotten; (2) As it is a district consolidated of several small districts into the county seat district circa 1970, true integration has been slow and only until very recently have old lines seemed to disappear.

In 2009, all indications were that the NACS was headed back into labor relations chaos. A new superintendent had just been hired. He inherited a district with certified staff working without a contract, three new board members—two of whom had been appointed due to others leaving the district and the other a former principal within the district—and about twenty labor grievances on his desk. I was an appointed board member from one of these consolidated districts. The opinions offered here come from this perspective and context.

In retrospect, the relationship between the faculty and the administration had deteriorated to the equivalent of a dysfunctional marriage. Neither party respected or cared to listen to the opinion of the other any longer. Undesirable intentions and behaviors were assumed. Adding to the difficulty was the poor reputation of the faculty representation as being quite unreasonable.

The three new board members were thrust into this toxic environment with a brand new superintendent and two other long-tenured board members who had tired of the continuous bickering. It was really quite a testament to the resolve of many individuals in the faculty, administration, and community that the educational level of the district remained at the levels it had come to expect.

The first year of my board experience was chaotic. The learning curve, already quite steep what with the various acronyms and idiosyncrasies of the various associated systems, was blurred by the ever-present labor relations issues. The former principal and I served on the contract negotiating team; deliberations could be characterized as adversarial and bizarre. The spokespersons were the prototypical board attorney and union representative grandstanding for their respective constituents.

Without effective, genuine communication, negotiations only became more acrimonious with each side reporting to their bodies the unresponsiveness of the other. It became apparent that another means of communication was needed. Out of this realization the humble beginnings of a shared leadership model were born.

Collectively over a few months, with then another new board member who had experience working with organized labor in a factory setting, the board settled on attempting to reach a goal of communicating directly with the teaching staff. We also resolved to create an atmosphere whereby the first call over a perceived slight or injustice was to the appropriate administrator rather than the union representative. Toward that end, the board proposed a board-level grievance step prior to arbitration. This was presented honestly to the collective bargaining unit as an attempt to ascertain truth.

If our administrators were really as problematic as the union representatives asserted, we could hear their story directly. A few veteran faculty members persuaded the union to take a chance with the new board, accepted the offer on the grievance protocol, and resolved to work out grievance issues privately as opposed to progressing through the arbitration process in order to save the district money and test the board's sincerity and, very frankly, attempt to salvage any shred of community reputation.

The next six months were eventful. Many of the minor grievances were quickly resolved. Most of the rest were resolved with considerable dialogue. It became apparent that the faculty, as much as anything, needed to experience an administration that would genuinely listen to their ideas. Eventually, all were resolved at a small fraction of the estimated cost.

Concurrently, one new grievance was filed and reached the board level. The dispute involved the superintendent, and the board representatives ruled in favor of the faculty. The superintendent, whose tenure had been less than stellar, became embittered toward the board. Within a few months, the board saw no recourse but to part company.

The board, realizing that a more approachable administration was crucial to any future success, needed to somehow find a superintendent with such a philosophy. Finding an external candidate would prove difficult due to the district history of labor turmoil. One veteran school principal exhibited collaborative leadership skills and had somehow survived the situation with a positive reputation with the staff. The district was blessed when the principal agreed to step up as superintendent.

One of the very first initiatives undertaken by the new district leader was to install a shared leadership initiative with the assistance of the state department of education. It involved the formation of a district leadership team (DLT) under which were formed building leadership teams (BLTs). There was approximately one faculty member per grade level along with all primary administrators on the DLT. Persuading faculty to serve on this initial DLT was no easy task. The same few veterans who persuaded the union to attempt collaboration served and helped persuade others to join.

The first meetings were facilitated by Ohio Department of Education (ODE) representatives. The faculty members appeared quite dubious and frankly almost fearful about this new concept. Ideas of one person, one vote; complete absence of retribution; insistence of open and honest discussion; implementation of decisions when board action was not required; and valuing and respecting each opinion were antithetical to their experience.

As the board representative, I observed a palpable sense of skepticism. The faculty members, for the most part, had not known anything other than top-down management with a heavy dose of retribution for challenging administration. The ODE representatives repeatedly emphasized the norms as the system was explained, while administrators and board representatives insisted they would be followed. But trust was going to be earned, not given.

Initial progress was confined to faculty and administration getting acquainted in a peer setting while they both learned more about the raw data of the district. Basically, the faculty was being exposed to the world of administration, while both were tentatively deliberating potential tactics of delivery and remediation. A few of the veteran faculty members gradually allowed themselves vulnerability, and trust was painstakingly tested and earned. The first year ended with little more than a tentative district plan and a willingness to regroup the next year and press on.

Subsequent meetings the next couple of years were eventful, emotional, and productive in fits and spurts. The faculty gradually learned that indeed the administration would act upon the recommendations of the DLT. Once trust was grudgingly given, the faculty had to learn to accept accountability, unfortunately a new concept to some of their worlds. This accountability, however, was intended to be conducted in a supportive and understanding environment.

Leadership skills needed to be developed on all fronts. Some administrators would occasionally act out of collaborative character and were called to accountability. Faculty gradually learned to deliberate complex decisions with fiscal responsibility. Over the course of about three years, the committees became functional.

As a participant, observer, and collaborative leader, I encountered many emotional experiences. On several occasions, the growth in the relationships and morale was so dramatic that I was overcome with happy tears on my way home from meetings. This growth occurred from administrators realizing the rather dramatic improvement in morale. The faculty took an increasing amount of ownership, and the district educational performance improved despite declining enrollments. The change in atmosphere and morale was nothing short of remarkable.

Lest the reader get the impression that such a model is a panacea for labor relations and improved performance, we must have discourse to the impediments to such a model. We are basically stalled to further improvement by several forces external to the district—state and federal mandates.

A lengthy discussion regarding financial constraints can be summed up succinctly—continual additional requirements delivered from the federal or state level with either little additional financial support or quite often with cuts. Most communities can bear no more. This nearly continuous flow of requirements and restrictions is tremendously demoralizing. A further hindrance to any collaborative model is the time commitment. Of course time is indeed a cost, but clearly diminished performance is costly, as well.

Local communities have become cynical and distrustful of the system. We see the movement of those families with resources moving to private school systems even when the public systems are quite effective. This is a loss both financially and culturally to the districts.

The litany of regulations becomes quite confusing and irrelevant to the citizenry.

The implementation and effects of mandates are often erroneously blamed by citizens on the local district, resulting in dissatisfaction with performance. This shifts an additional segment toward private schools, which in turn reduced state and federal aid. The confusion also costs the districts at the ballot box and therefore the treasury. It is extremely difficult to explain to communities with minimal resources the benefits of time and money spent on a collaborative leadership model.

Another unpopular discussion point, and the last we will belabor, is the current legal structure of labor relations. The systems of organized labor for certified staff are classic adversarial systems. Often some of our collaborative possibilities are nixed at the organized labor level. It is understandable given the constraints and mindset instituted under such a system. It is the subtle and subconscious effect this system has on the individuals within its jurisdiction.

There is no incentive to be innovative or excellent, and often by peer pressure such is frowned upon. I see time and again how this subtly constrains our very talented staff. A victim or entitlement mentality, especially given the current political assault on standards and regulation, is again quietly and sometimes not so quietly asserted and reinforced.

Organized labor may be unwilling to make collaborative concessions at the local level due to the setting of precedent or appearance of weakness on a larger stage. The vast majority of our staff are talented and motivated and want to do well for children. The collaborative model enhances cooperation and naturally encourages positive pressure. However, when innovation runs near proximity to any negotiated labor agreement, innovation loses.

In summation, our experience realized significant benefits to a shared leadership model for education. The positives were both tangible (performance) and less tangible (morale and community support). However, these benefits are currently constrained by heavy-handed intrusion from state and federal authorities, resulting confusion and turmoil at the local level, and the current legal structure of the workforce. I believe mitigation of these restrictions could have a phenomenal positive influence to the potential accomplishments of a shared leadership model.

UNITED SAM

On the long bus ride home, Sam had plenty of time to reflect on the trip and her discussion with Catherine. She pulled out her tablet and began to scan through her notes with highlights from several of our nation's founding documents. While she was deep in thought, she felt a tapping on her shoulder. It was Willis Davidson trying to get her attention.

"Ms. Levy, when we get back to school next week, can a few of us meet with you to talk about student involvement in decision making?" Elizabeth and Kyle were in the neighboring seat and cast cautious eyes in her direction.

"I'll be happy to meet with you guys, just as long as it's not a formal meeting with the Student Council. So if the meeting is just with the four of us, let's do it."

The three students were happy to start the conversation. Sam was somewhat apprehensive. She didn't know where this would go, nor what the students really wanted. One thing was for sure, she needed to start some kind of conversation with some faculty members. That would be on the top of her "to-do" list for Monday.

Back on her tablet, Samantha sketched out ideas from the founding documents that seemed germane to democratic schools. At first blush, the list looked more limited than she was expecting, but overwhelming in terms of what changes it might portend.

Five Core Democratic Values

1. Liberty
2. Common Good
3. Justice
4. Equality
5. Diversity

Four Constitutional Principles

1. Rule of Law
2. Separation of Powers
3. Representative Government
4. Checks and Balances

Declaration of Independence

1. All men are created equal.
2. Leaders receive their power from their constituents.

United States Constitution

Article I (Legislative Branch)
Section 1: Describes that all legislative powers are vested in Congress (Senate and House of Representatives)—[Representation and Balance of Power].
Section 4: Congress assembles at least once per year.
Section 5: Record and publish proceedings of meetings.
Section 6: No person can hold office in two branches.
Section 7: Bills must pass both Houses and the President; can be overturned with 2/3 vote of Congress.

Article II (Executive Branch)
Section 1: Describes Executive Power in the person of the President.
Section 3: President reports to Congress from time to time.

Article III (Judicial Branch)
Section 1: Describes Supreme Court and is a place for people to air their grievances—[Balance of Power and Checks and Balances].
Bill of Rights: First 10 Amendments to the Constitution.
First Amendment: Freedom of Speech and Assembly, and the ability to challenge government's decisions.

As the bus pulled into the Washington High School parking lot, Samantha wanted to stop thinking about this possible undertaking. Besides, she had to make sure the kids got picked up by their parents. Two things were for certain: She was going to meet with some of her more open-minded teachers on Monday, and she had to meet with those students. And two things were uncertain: Who were those teachers, and what would they say?

It was 3:15 on Monday afternoon; classes were done for the day. Jose Perez, Greta McGovern, and Gene Jones joined Sam around her small conference room table. Gene was the first teacher Sam hired at Washington. He was a veteran theatre teacher and came to New LaCerne with his wife Patty when she took an IT management position in a local corporate office. Gene enjoyed life but was never satisfied with the way things were. He always questioned everything, it seemed. In her mind, Sam liked what Gene could bring to the table, but he would be a "wild card."

Sam began the meeting by recounting the class trip to the nation's capital. Jose added points along the way. He spent some time detailing the conversation with the students, and Sam concluded with a rather lengthy description of her conversations with Catherine Beyers. She had copies of her typed notes, but she decided not to share them at this time.

She looked around the table to see what kind of reactions she got from her colleagues. A three-second pause seemed like an eternity, but Gene was the first to respond. "What are you looking for from us, Samantha? Are you suggesting we become a democratic school?"

Greta chimed in. "I'm not sure what you want. Do you have something in mind?"

Jose squinted his eyes at Samantha. He wasn't sure what to make of this conversation, either.

Samantha decided to jump in with both feet. She shared her notes. The small group chatted about these notes for roughly forty-five minutes. It was decided that Samantha would begin to put some sort of framework together and share in two weeks. There was some excitement, but it seemed to Sam that there was more skepticism than she anticipated. Her biggest surprise came from her wild card as everyone was getting up to leave.

"Let's remember that real reform comes from the people, not those at the top. I hope I'm not coming across critically, but I really want to know why we're doing this. Who gains? What's the purpose? What are the expectations? Let's ponder these questions so we can talk about them when we next meet." With that Gene nodded his head and gave a calm smile.

As promised, Sam bought box lunches for her three students. They each sat around the conference room table where Samantha met with her faculty colleagues the afternoon before.

Really, it was because of the students' short lunch schedule that the meeting got focused quickly. Willis began, "Thank you for meeting with us, Ms. Levy. I apologize if we seem eager to get going with some ideas, but I'm a senior, and so is Elizabeth. We're short-timers here, and we'd like to do something of significance this year."

Samantha nodded her head. "I understand. First, though, I'd like to hear what you're thinking about."

Elizabeth continued. "Well, we don't want to waste your time, so we prepared some notes. We talked with Mr. Perez. He said you met with him yesterday."

Samantha was taken aback by this comment. She wanted that to be a personal conversation with her faculty colleagues. Jose should not have mentioned it to the students. She made a mental note to talk with him later about confidentiality.

Elizabeth went on. "We think students should be able to vote on some things that are important to our education. For example, we think that we should have a voice in hiring teachers and maybe who gets raises and who gets fired."

Samantha swallowed hard. Kyle took his turn. "Ms. Levy, we also think we maybe should have some say in what classes are taught and even the schedule of the day—you know, when classes begin and when the day ends."

Willis saved the best for last. "Most of all, Ms. Levy, we don't simply think that having certain voting privileges is sufficient, but we believe that a formal structure is appropriate. In other words, we think that students need a seat at the table."

Samantha had listened to all this carefully with her hands folded on the table. Truly, she didn't know what to say, but she knew these young adults were awaiting her response. "I'm interested in what you're asking of me. I'm going to have to give this some careful deliberation. Please give me some time to cogitate and get back to you."

While Samantha hoped that would be good enough, it wasn't. Willis asked, "When can we meet next? Also, we'd like to invite you to our next Student Council meeting—this Thursday."

Samantha's eyes must have been wide open. She knew she had to get in control of this before things got out of hand. Thankfully, at that very moment there was a knock on her door. It was Jose Perez.

Sam didn't even get out of her conference table chair as the students filed out and Jose poked his head around her office door. "Jose, we have to get these kids under control."

"My goodness, Sam, what did they say?"

"They want me to meet with the Student Council on Thursday!" Samantha exclaimed in an incredulous tone.

"Oh, that's all?" came Jose's response.

"Well, I'm not ready to meet with them. I have a lot of thinking to do before I'm prepared to meet with the student government."

"No problem," replied Jose. "I'll tell them that you are unable to meet this week but that you'll get back to them in the near future."

With that Samantha got up and walked to the parking lot with Jose.

As they arrived at her car, Jose put his hand on Samantha's shoulder. "We're in this together, Sam. We are expecting great things from you; we told you that when we interviewed you. But, again, we're in this together. See you tomorrow."

Samantha had stopped at the local Chinese restaurant, Wok Inn, on her way home. So now she sat in her recliner, put on HGTV, and ate her pan-fried dumplings. She felt guilty, but she needed a break.

An hour later, she was able to shake off her quiet desperation and grabbed a notepad that she always kept next to her favorite chair and began to jot down notes in a stream of consciousness:

- Create a system where faculty and staff and parents feel and actually do have real input into decision making.
- Do students have a role? If so, what role?
- How do you create a system that encourages broad participation yet uses the expertise of the professional educators?
- How will my role change?
- How do I start the conversation and with whom?
- What would be the three branches? Principal? Site Council? Supreme Court?
- Don't create a new bureaucracy or an overwhelming series of bylaws and rules.
- Keep in mind: Separation of Powers, Representative Government, Checks and Balances.

- How do you get true representation?
- How do I maintain at least veto power?
- Who sets the budget and policies?

She began to outline a framework. . . . This weekend she was going to put together a Prezi presentation; she would first show it to some faculty and staff members and get their feedback. After that, she would share a modified version with the Student Council.

KEY POINTS

- Typical top-down models of change will not work for the cultural shift necessary for shared decision making; collaborative change models focusing on people and process are required.
- Concerns about democratic decision making can be categorized as fear of others' motives, fear of new power structures/loss of power, fear of being held accountable, fear of lack of time, and fear of conflict.
- There are five essential core values of democratic organizations: (1) liberty, (2) common good, (3) justice, (4) equality, and (5) diversity.
- There are four essential constitutional principles of democratic organizations: (1) rule of law, (2) separation of powers, (3) representative government, and (4) checks and balances.

POINTS TO PONDER

1. What types of concerns or fears will people at your school have about the type of change being discussed here?
2. What would the five essential core values look like in practice at your school?
3. What would the four essential constitutional principles look like in practice at your school?
4. What would the three governing branches of a school look like in terms of membership and responsibilities?

NOTES

1. Fritjof Capra, *The Hidden Connections: A Science of Sustainable Living* (New York: Anchor Books, 2004), 34.

2. Charles Heckscher, "Defining the Post-Bureaucratic Type," in Charles Heckscher and Lynda Applegate, eds., *The Post-Bureaucratic Organization: New Perspectives on Organizational Change* (Thousand Oaks, CA: Sage, 1994), 23.

3. Ibid., 24.

4. Richard H. Wells and J. Steven Picou, "The Becoming Place: A Study of Educational Change in a Small College," *Research in Higher Education* 17(1), (1982): 29.

5. Charles Heckscher, R. Eisenstat, and T. Rice, "Transformational Processes," in Charles Heckscher and Lynda Applegate, eds., *The Post-Bureaucratic Organization: New Perspectives on Organizational Change* (Thousand Oaks, CA: Sage, 1994), 147.

6. Ibid., Capra, 103.

7. Ibid., Wells and Picou, 28.

8. Ibid., 29.

9. Ibid., Heckscher, Eisenstat, and Rice, "Transformational Processes," 136.

10. Francis X. Neumann Jr., "Organizational Structures to Match the New Information-Rich Environments: Lessons Learned from the Study of Chaos," in *Public Productivity and Management Review* 21(1) (September 1997): 95.

11. James G. March and Johan P. Olsen. *Democratic Governance* (New York: The Free Press, 1995), 185–86. The authors continue to explain three other ways systems change: "Radical transformations are associated with major performance crises resulting from substantial changes in the environment and creeping obsolescence of stable systems. . . . Internal Dynamics—Political institutions also change through mundane internal processes. . . . Co-evolution of Environments and Institutions—Changes in institutions are not unique adaptations to exogenous environmental pressures and internal dynamics but sequences of steps summarizing interactions between external forces and internal processes. Change involved mutual learning and co-evolution" (186–89).

12. Ibid., Francis X. Neumann Jr., 95.

13. Ibid., March and Olsen, 194.

14. Ibid., Heckscher, Eisenstat, and Rice, 136–37.

15. George Packer, *The Fight Is for Democracy* (New York: Harper Collins, 2003), 6.

16. Items 2–7 come from Susan E. Mundry and Leslie F. Hergert, eds., *Making Change for School Improvement* (Andover, MA: The Network, Inc., 1988), 23–24.

17. Items 1–4 come from Susan E. Mundry and Leslie F. Hergert eds., *Making Change for School Improvement* (Andover, MA: The Network, Inc., 1988), 25–26.

18. Ibid., Mundry and Hergert, 28–29. Citing the work of D. Crandall, et al., *A Study of Dissemination Efforts Supporting School Improvement* (Andover, MA: The Network, Inc., 1982).

19. Anne Donnellon and Maureen Scully, "Teams, Performance, and Rewards: Will the Post-Bureaucratic Organization Be a Post-Meritocratic Organization?" in Charles Heckscher and Lynda Applegate, eds., *The Post-Bureaucratic Organization: New Perspectives on Organizational Change* (Thousand Oaks, CA: Sage, 1994), 70. In a most fascinating discussion Nohria and Berkley explained, "In this new corporate world of blurred boundaries, ubiquitous technology, and 'empowered' individuals, what counts as an organization? Given these examples, what once seemed stable and self-evident about the very idea of 'the organization' now appears obscure and rather arbitrary." Nitin Nohria and James D. Berkley, "The Virtual Organization: Bureaucracy, Technology, and the Implosion of Control," in ibid., Heckscher and Applegate, 110.

20. Ibid., March and Olsen, 192.

21. Edward S. Greenberg, *Workplace Democracy: The Political Effects of Participation* (Ithaca, NY: Cornell University Press, 1986), 28. For a most insightful and exhaustive review of the loss of democracy in the workplace, the reader is invited to examine Howard Zinn's book, *Declarations of Independence: Cross-Examining American Ideology* (New York: HarperCollins, 1990).

22. George Cheney et al., "Democracy, Participation, and Communication at Work: A Multidisciplinary Review," *Communication Yearbook* 21 (2004): 54.

23. Zelda Gamson and Henry Levin, "Obstacles to the Survival of Democratic Organizations," in Robert Jackall and Henry M. Levin, eds., *Worker Cooperatives in America* (Berkeley, CA: University of California Press, 1984), 223. For additional information on worker cooperatives, the reader is invited to investigate Worker Cooperatives, *Community-Wealth.org* at http://community-wealth.org.

24. William E. Halal, *The New Management: Bringing Democracy and Markets Inside Organizations* (San Francisco: Berrett-Koehler, 1998), 93.

25. Peter Bachrach and Aryeh Botwinick, *Power and Empowerment: A Radical Theory of Participatory Democracy* (Philadelphia: Temple University Press, 1992), 103.

26. John Smyth, "The Socially Just Alternative to the 'Self-Managing School,'" in Keith Leithwood et al., eds., *International Handbook of Educational Leadership and Administration* (The Netherlands: Kluwer Academic Publishers, 1996), 1097. Smyth also explains that governing bodies maintain priority setting and leave the detail work for the teachers, and call it empowerment. Furthermore, requisite resources for sites to carry out their decisions are seriously limited, giving them little practical power.

27. Howard Zinn, *Declarations of Independence: Cross-Examining American Ideology* (New York: Harper Collins, 1990), 219.

28. Paulo Freire, *Pedagogy of the Oppressed* (New York: Continuum, 1970), 45.

29. Maxim Voronov and Peter T. Coleman, "Beyond the Ivory Towers: Organizational Power Practices and a 'Practical' Critical Postmodernism," *The Journal of Applied Behavioral Science,* 39(2) (June 2003): 173.

30. Fareed Zakaria, *The Future of Freedom: Illiberal Democracy at Home and Abroad* (New York: W. W. Norton & Company, 2003), 102. Drawing similar conclusions to the workplace, Gordon stipulated, "Some social theorists . . . have observed that groups, even devoutly democratic ones, seem to evolve into an oligarchical structure, with power relinquished by the majority to a small handful of 'leaders.'" Frederick Gordon, "Bureaucracy: Can We Do Better? Can We Do Worse?" in ibid., Heckscher and Applegate, 215.

31. Ibid., Voronov and Coleman, 176.

32. Samuel Huntington, *The Clash of Civilizations: Remaking of World Order* (New York: Simon & Schuster, 1997), 71.

33. Ibid.

34. Ibid., March and Olsen, 55.

35. Ibid., Bachrach and Botwinick, 164.

36. Teresa M. Harrison, "Designing the Post-Bureaucratic Organization: Toward Egalitarian Organizational Structure," *Australian Journal of Communication,* 19(2) (1992): 20.

37. Ibid., Smyth, 1100.

38. Ibid., Greenberg, 32.

39. Ibid., Greenberg, 32.

40. Ibid., Cheney et al., 63.

41. Peter Block, *Stewardship: Choosing Service over Self-Interest* (San Francisco: Berrett-Koehler, 1996), 238. Ibid., Cheney et al., 64, mirrored this message: "Within the context of organized labor, voice as a practical construct refers to autonomous practices of speech that are braced by institutional guarantees. The right of free speech guaranteed to U.S. citizens by the First Amendment largely disappears within the context of the workplace; the Bill of Rights does not protect workers from private sector abuses. Laws that govern

speech-related rights within the context of organized labor are thus rooted in an amazingly complicated mixture of Supreme Court rulings, National Labor Relations Board rulings, union constitutions, and agreements made during the course of collective bargaining."

42. Ibid., Greenberg, 170.

43. Ibid., Charles Heckscher, 39. Heckscher details these two principles:

> The bureaucratic type relies on what Weber calls "rational-legal" legitimation: Orders are accepted as valid if they conform to the impersonal rules defining appropriate powers of an office. The *content* [emphasis in original] of those orders is explicitly not subject to examination by subordinates—as long as it comes through proper channels and in the proper form it is to be obeyed. . . . An elaborate system of checks and balances and rights is the way consensual legitimation is guaranteed.

Heckscher continues,

> [t]he process can be boiled down to three essential elements: (1) bringing together stakeholders; (2) creating a dialogue; and (3) achieving consensus on a path forward. When bringing stakeholders together, the people with the most expertise and who are affected by the decision are the ones involved—not necessarily people of formal positions. In order to maintain accountability and to get the work done, such groups must focus on creating explicit detailing of expected outcomes . . . conscious reflection on process . . . and carefully document the decisions that are made and to assign responsibility. . . . The integration of a post-bureaucratic order requires not that every decision go through a consensus process but that every decision be made according to principles that have been developed through such a process. That is, there should be access for stakeholders to the definition of the basic goals and values of each decision area. . . . Finally, in a changing order there will continually be decisions that do not clearly fall under principles already agreed to: This is where the "meta-decision-making-structures" described above—structures for "deciding how to decide"—must enter the picture, to establish a new process for making the decision and creating guidelines for the new domain (39–41).

44. The discussion of core values of the American Constitution and Constitutional Principles were taken from CIVITAS: *A Frame Work for Civic Education*, a collaborative project of the Center for Civic Education and the Council for the Advancement of Citizenship, National Council for the Social Studies Bulletin, No. 86, 1991. Borrowed from www.constitutioncenter.org/explore/TheUS.Constitution/index.shtml. The core values are cited from page 1 and the constitutional principles from page 2. For additional insights into the principles of democracy, the reader is invited to visit https://web.stanford.edu/~ldiamond/iraq/DemocracyEducation0204.htm by Larry Diamond. The

reader is also invited to visit the website of the Library of Congress at www.loc.gov/law/help/guide/federal/usconst.php.

45. Ibid., Huntington, 110.

46. Ibid., Zakaria, 157.

47. Ibid., March and Olsen, 22. James March and Johan Olsen quote the work of Dahl. "For example, Dahl (1980) mentions several fundamental rights and rules necessary for a democratic process: open inquiry, discussion, enlightened understanding, equal consideration, effective participation, and a decision reached by some system of voting that respects the essential equality of the citizens."

48. Ibid., Edward S. Greenberg. Greenberg stipulated that equality, dispersal of power, and democratic planning are necessary characteristics of a democratic society. I would argue that we could extend "democratic planning" to mean "democratic processes" and "democratic society" to "democratic systems."

49. D. Dotlich and P. Cairo, *Unnatural Leadership: Going Against Intuition and Experience to Develop Ten New Leadership Instincts* (San Francisco: Jossey-Bass, 2002), 162. "Empowerment in complex organizations, however, is essential; it's impossible to compete and grow if the people who are furthest from the customers are making the decisions. Leaders need to trust that those on the front line are in the best position to make decisions." To which Atkinson added, "The management principles of democracy, profit-sharing, and information require a collegial approach to sharing information and decision-making. The conventional top-down flows of information, decision-making authority, and responsibility give way to an environment where the opinion of the *knowledge worker* (emphasis in original) is valued, sought out, and considered." Anthony Atkinson, "The Promise of Employee Involvement," in *CMA Magazine* 3 (April 1990): 8.

50. Ibid., Bachrach and Botwinick, 41. "Within a participatory society equality of power was intended to replace hierarchy." These same authors later detailed this point: "What is required at this juncture is an alternative vision which effectively connects the concrete concerns, needs, and anxieties of working-class people with what they would consider to be their democratic right to share equally, as individuals, in decision making on all levels of the enterprise in which they work. Their right to participate in the workplace should be formulated as one of their essential political rights. . . This concept of the right of participation should be broadly conceived as something that all democratic citizens have in common, whether as residents of communities or as workers locked into business, professional, or governmental bureaucracies" (163).

51. Democracies require diversity of people participating and sharing their opinions, and democratic organizations need flexibility in operationalizing

their values. But "participation is not equivalent to democracy," E. Davis and Russell Lansbury, *Democracy and Control in the Workplace* (Melbourne, Australia: Longman Cheshire, 1986), 35. "Democracy thrives on instruments for creating and maintaining diversity. It profits from public criticism and debate, from conflict over values and rules, and from differences that lead to experimentation with alternative practices and exploration of new visions," ibid., March and Olsen, *Democratic Governance,* 1995, 169. To which Jackall and Crain added, "One of the keys to maintaining a democratic work situation is to foster an organizational spontaneity—that is, a responsiveness to new ideas, a willingness to break up routines when they become problematic, or indeed to change whole organizational arrangements to fit workers' needs and aspirations." See "The Contemporary Small Cooperative Movement" in Robert Jackall and Henry Levin, *Worker Cooperatives in America* (Berkeley, CA: University of California Press, 1984), 100.

52. Trust, openness, and honesty are essential characteristics of any functioning democratic institution. Eminent historian Howard Zinn warns us, "When the government acts in secrecy, free speech is thwarted, and democracy undermined." Ibid., Zinn, 220. Another eminent historian, Samuel Huntington, declared, "The absence of trust in the culture of the society provides formidable obstacles to the creation of public institutions." Ibid., Huntington, 28.

53. Ibid., March and Olsen, 150–52. "In democratic theory, responsibility refers to being answerable to somebody else and having to account for one's actions or inactions and their consequences. . . . The ability of citizens to hold policy-makers accountable and the ability to hold bureaucrats accountable are standard premises of democracy." Therefore, holding elected officials and bureaucrats accountable is the responsibility of the individual citizens and workers.

54. Ibid., *Civitas, A Framework for Civic Education,* 1991.

55. Ibid., *Civitas.*

56. Ibid., March and Olsen, 126. "[Rules] define how authority is created, exercised, transferred, and made responsible."

57. Ibid., 224.

58. Hilary Wainwright, *Reclaim the State: Experiments in Popular Democracy* (London: Verso, 2003), 188–89.

59. Ibid., Cheney et al., 40.

60. Ibid., 61. These authors go on to write, "Ultimately, then, workplace or organizational democracy should be understood in terms of a wide range of communication practices. . . And, given that these very practices may be seen as constituting democracy, they must be open-ended, adaptable, and subject to scrutiny" (88).

61. Ibid, March and Olsen, 22.

CHAPTER 4

Implications and Applications for Our Schools

To this point in the book, we have focused on how modern organizations developed and the underlying assumptions upon which they have been built. We then examined fundamental principles of democratic organizations. It is now time for us to focus our attention to a discussion of contemporary structures of democratic institutions in this postmodern world.

As we begin to examine governance models, however, we should reemphasize the benefits of shifting from our authoritarian, control-oriented institutions to more egalitarian, open organizations. Moreover, it is critical to lay the appropriate foundation and requisite conditions for the creation of democratic organizations.

Let us begin with the mention of two examples of organizations that have some experience with democratic practices. One is a public school system and the other is from the private sector. In an effort to gain citizen support of their local schools, Chicago officials created a deliberative process to significantly involve community members and families in decisions that impacted their lives.

In the Pacific Northwest, a number of logging companies have a long history of employee ownership and involvement in decision making at what have become known as worker cooperatives. (The reader is invited to read the descriptive analysis of these examples as referenced in the back of this chapter.)

While the lasting success of these efforts may be debatable, the benefits of such approaches are clear. In their exhaustive investigation of the Chicago Public School System, Archon Fung and Erik Olin

Wright have identified several instrumental advantages of democratic organizations.

- The individuals most closely tied "to the points of action, and who possess intimate knowledge about relevant situations" are empowered to think, plan, and act.
- These same individuals "may also know how best to improve the situation."
- "The deliberative process that regulates these groups' decision making is likely to generate superior solutions compared to hierarchical . . . procedures."
- Democratic processes "shorten the feedback loop—the distance between decision, action, effect, observation, and reconsideration . . . and so create a nimble style of collective activity that can recognize and respond to erroneous or ineffective strategies."
- New and flexible "component groups" are formed. "This proliferation of command points allows multiple strategies, techniques, and priorities to be pursued simultaneously in order more rapidly to discover and diffuse those that prove themselves to be most effective."[1]

In his work studying the worker cooperatives in the plywood corporations of the American Northwest, Edward Greenberg noted that employees who have the opportunity to work in democratic workplaces "are active and informed participants in those informal decisional processes by which work is organized and executed."[2] Not only are they informed participants, but they actually initiate change and innovations.[3]

Worker cooperative experts Jackall and Crain resonate with these benefits to democratic workplaces. "We want to stress the profound motivating quality of these experiences. Despite the many problems of worker cooperatives, they offer a unique place in our society for many young people to taste actual self-determination, ownership of productive capital, and the singular joy of seeing one's self and one's deepest values expressed in one's work."[4]

Further, democratic organizations expect more autonomy and freedom for their workers. With these freedoms, on the other hand, comes full responsibility.[5] In other words, workers cannot expect to have freedom and authority without the commensurate responsibilities that come along with their decision making.

While there are notable cases of such change coming from those in positions of authority, such examples are few. We should not expect change to be initiated from those on top of the hierarchy. When change is propelled from the top, it has been forced upon them by active citizens and workers. True sustained and substantive change comes from the grassroots level.

Howard Zinn eloquently made this case in his seminal work, *Declaration of Independence: Cross-Examining American Ideology*. Zinn cited the Abolitionist Movement. Politicians passed legislation only after overwhelming pressures by the people. The same can be said about reforms created by the New Deal, the National Labor Relations Act, Civil Rights, indeed the American Revolution, student uprising in Tiananmen Square in China, and the Arab Spring in the Middle East.

Zinn specified, "It seems that very many people understand the existence of injustice and the need for change. But they consider themselves helpless, and this is probably the greatest obstacle to social change. . . . Those victories for social justice did not come from the normal workings of the political system. It is useful, even necessary, to work through the regular channels as far as they can take you. But they have never taken us very far."[6]

These historical examples are poignant and powerful. Yet they serve as examples for contemporary grassroots movements for change, in general, and for democratic change, in particular.

Numerous scholars have created a composite list of requisite conditions for contemporary practices in democratic organizations. For example, Teresa Harrison states, "The issue raised for organizational communication scholars is how to design a structure that integrates wider participation and provides for the expertise required for effective decision making."[7]

What kinds of organizational structures need to be in place in order to create a model of shared decision making? The new sciences provide direction in laying the foundation for contemporary democratic organizations. From these new sciences we learn that dynamic flexibility is a requirement. Dissipative structures would serve as a highly appropriate metaphor.

"We have also learned from the new sciences that interconnected relationships are central to all systems. Rather than build rigid hierarchies, we must create webs of relationships both internal and external to the organizations. These relationships must be fluid and flexible to adapt quickly to change and to continue to grow."[8] We will need to rely less on formal structures and provide more opportunity for informal networks. People need to be able to communicate across the system openly and transparently.

According to Charles Heckscher,

> [t]he central theoretical claim of a post-bureaucratic organization is that it is possible to make binding decisions without relying on offices. This claim in turn relies on two concepts unfamiliar to bureaucracy: consensual legitimation and process.... The conception of consensual legitimacy is new to organizational theory, but it is old in other contexts: It is known as democracy. The founders of the American republic, and to a certain extent even the authors of the Magna Carta, appealed to this form of legitimation. In the former case it became institutionalized in the system of government defined in our Constitution—an elaborate system of checks and balances and rights.[9]

When people begin to debureaucratize their organizations, they have to trust in the process. "The process can be boiled down to three essential elements:

1. Bringing together stakeholders;
2. Creating a dialogue; and
3. Achieving consensus on a path forward."[10]

However, restructuring our organizations to be more democratic, egalitarian, and adaptive does not mean a total dismantling of our existing systems. According to Neumann,

> [t]he answer would seem to balance deterministic structural elements with those that are more stochastic in nature, that is, by blending hierarchical structures with more network-like structures.... Together, they comprise a healthy organization. The adaptive organization in a postindustrial world would, then, best respond to its increasingly complex and information-laden environment not necessarily by casting off its bureau-

cratic structure and beginning to behave as, for example, a spontaneous network; rather, its most effective response would be to absorb some of the external complexity to produce a random, or stochastic, counterbalance to its existing linear, or deterministic, characteristics.[11]

So again, it's not a black-and-white, either/or way of thinking. Rather, it is a gray, both/and type of thinking of organizational structures. Bureaucratic structures need to be enhanced with shared decision-making processes and practices.

Any organization that would be considered to be democratic must be collaborative in its decision making and reduce the cumbersome hierarchies that impede free flow of information and thinking. Management expert William Halal wrote, "Modern organizations master complexity by having entrepreneurial units manage themselves from the bottom up."

Rather than clinging to rigid hierarchies, Halal explained that "The most feasible successor to the hierarchy currently is the concept of 'organizational networks.' In this model, contemporary teams use groupware to form strategic alliances, producing a fluid network that can mobilize to meet changing market needs quickly."[12]

Noted natural scientist Fritjof Capra also talks of a need for balance between bureaucratic structures and organic structures. He calls these "designed structures" and "emergent structures," respectively. These two types of structures are very different, and every organization needs both kinds:

> Designed structures provide the rules and routines that are necessary for the effective functioning of the organization. . . . Designed structures provide stability. Emergent structures, on the other hand, provide novelty, creativity, and flexibility. They are adaptive, capable of changing and evolving. In today's complex business environment, purely designed structures do not have the necessary responsiveness and learning capability. They may be capable of magnificent feats, but since they are not adaptive, they are deficient when it comes to learning and changing, and thus likely to be left behind.[13]

Finally, as employees enjoy more freedoms and autonomy in this new model, there needs to be an increased demand for personal responsibility and accountability. In his study of the democratic transformations in the Chicago Public Schools Archon Fung coined the phrase "accountable-autonomy" model to describe the praxis of freedom with responsibility. "Accountable-autonomy reforms improve governance by reinforcing and making transparent patterns of communication and cooperation between community members and local officials."[14]

With all this said, it appears that a number of requisite conditions need to be understood when conceptualizing a model for shared governance. Before we examine such models, it would be prudent to list these conditions:

- A structure that encourages wide participation and relationships across the system;
- a structure that is flexible in terms of supporting communication both laterally and horizontally in the organization; and,
- a structure that empowers constituents but at the same time holds them accountable.

Now that we have identified these requisite conditions to empower stakeholders in our schools, it is time to explore structural elements required for democratic models.

THE DEMOCRATIC ORGANIZATION

After a tremendous amount of debate during the Philadelphia Convention, the American founding fathers drafted a constitution to be ratified by the states. Their struggles focused on such issues as balance of power, a system of checks and balances, and even the number of branches in the government. The role of the executive received a great deal of scrutiny. In the end, our three "branches" (executive, legislative, and judicial) were agreed upon (see table 4.1). Obviously, this was a political model. In the Industrial Age, the business world embraced a corporate model (see table 4.2). Patrick Dolan referred to these three branches as "anchors" (administration, union, and board).[15]

If we were to examine these two models, we would see that each has three primary authority groups, but their foci are dissimilar.

Table 4.1. Democratic Governance Model

Legislative	Executive	Judicial
Senate and House of Representatives • Creates the laws	President • Executes the laws	Supreme Court • Interprets the laws

With all its inherent foibles, the Democratic Governance Model does equalize the balance of power among all three branches and provides for a system of checks and balances so that one branch does not overreach its authority. The U.S. Constitution enumerates the checks on all three branches. As particularly germane to the focus of this book, the Legislative branch checks the Executive branch with the ability to override presidential vetoes. The Legislative branch checks the Judiciary branch by approving federal judges, and it has the ability to create constitutional amendments.

As the Legislative branch is a bicameral body, it also checks itself, since both Houses must pass bills, and these houses also initiate budgetary bills. The Executive branch checks the Legislative branch with its own veto authority, the vice president is president of the Senate, and it can call Congress into an emergency session. It checks the Judicial branch with the ability to appoint judges and with the authority to pardon.

The Executive branch has a self-regulating check by allowing the vice president and Cabinet to rule that the president is unfit to carry out his or her duties. Finally, the Judicial branch checks both the Executive and Legislative branches via the process of judicial review in order to make certain that neither branch is operating outside its scope of responsibilities.[16]

The Corporate Governance Model does not balance the power, nor does it necessarily provide for a satisfactory system of checks and balances to counter the power in each anchor. The Board of Trustees sets the vision and priorities; the CEO executes the vision and the priorities; and the unions protect the employees' rights. At best, this model checks

Table 4.2. Corporate Governance Model

Board of Trustees	Administration/CEO	Union/Workers
• Sets the vision	• Executes the vision	• Protects employee rights

Table 4.3. Higher Education Shared Governance Model

Board of Trustees	President/Chancellor	Faculty Senate
• Sets the vision	• Executes the vision	• Ensures faculty rights

itself through adversarial relationships—each anchor needs the other in order to exist in a quasi-symbiotic coexistence.

Colleges and universities, however, have established a model of shared governance that has served them well for many decades (see table 4.3). It is this derivative democratic model that could provide the most direct and pragmatic approach for K–12 schools to infuse our founding democratic principles into a shared governance model for real impact.

Colleges and universities will have an Executive embodied in a president or chancellor. It will also have a Board of Trustees or Board of Regents. However, its third branch is of particular interest here. The Faculty Senate houses the shared governance rights of the faculty. Some campuses will further these rights to other personnel via a Staff Senate. In any case, the Faculty Senate provides that vehicle for professors to be engaged in decision making pertinent to their professional domain.

Bowen and Tobin have written extensively on the governance model in higher education.[17] It is appropriate to spend a few moments discussing the roles and responsibilities of these three governing groups at American colleges and universities. Bowen and Tobin remind us of the "traditional faculty rights and responsibilities in the familiar areas of composition of faculty, curriculum, admissions, student life, and academic freedom."

However, they go on to discuss the American Association of University Professors (AAUP) position on roles and responsibilities: "Throughout its hundred-year history, the AAUP has consistently acknowledged that governing boards and administrations have primary authority over matters affecting institutions' mission, planning, financial resources, and budgeting. By the late 1960s, however, the AAUP had begun to assert the faculty's *consultative* [emphasis added] rights in all matters affecting college and university decision making."

In referencing Princeton University's shared governance policy, Bowen and Tobin explain, "The *Statement of Delegation* distinguishes among matters where the trustees exercise only 'general review' (e.g., faculty appointment processes, curricular decisions, and other academic matters), matters where trustees exercise 'prior review' (when there is a claim on funds, including the setting of budgets), and matters where there is 'authority directly exercised' by the trustees (investments, real estate transactions, and so on)."

Therefore, it is the Trustees' and the Administration' roles to establish vision, do strategic planning, and make broad fiscal and budgetary decisions, while faculty should have consultative roles in these areas. On the other hand, college faculty has primary responsibilities in faculty hiring/promotion/tenure, curriculum, admissions standards, student life, and academic freedom. Of course, administration is critically involved in each of these areas in our contemporary institutions. These associated responsibilities of professors, however, should serve as aspirant goals for democratic school teachers in the K–12 setting.

It is this Higher Education Model of Shared Governance, coupled with the Democratic Governance Model, that could perhaps provide a pragmatic structure for the governance of our schools. Let us refer to it as the Democratic School Governance Model (see table 4.4).

It should be noted that this is a *school* governance model and not a *district* or *school system* governance model. In a later discussion under Tier III, a district or school system model will be described.

For a moment, let us describe in better detail the responsibilities of each of these branches or anchors in a Democratic School Governance Model. The "Executive branch" is led by the principal, of course. The "Legislative branch" is made up of two groups. The first group would be the Faculty Senate, made up of some preapportioned faculty representation. It may also have a nonvoting membership to include student, nonfaculty staff, and parent representation. The office of the principal

Table 4.4. Democratic School Governance Model

Site Council and Faculty Senate	Principal	District Council
• Sets vision/policies	• Executes vision/policies • Ensures anchors operate within their scope of authority	• Resolves disputes between anchors

may serve in an ex-officio role, or the assistant principal might serve as chair.

The second legislative group or Site Council, akin to a House of Representatives, would include faculty representation, staff representation, parent and community representation, and possibly student representation. The ratio could be proportional or equal. It would be important that underrepresented populations—be they ethnic, socioeconomic status, etc.—have representation. Again, the office of the principal could hold an ex-officio role.

The third branch or anchor group may be the most novel and controversial. This "Judicial branch" or District Council would have authority to resolve disputes if it chooses. It would need representation of faculty and staff, parents and community members, school board members, and district-level and building-level administration chosen by the other anchors.

Individuals on the District Council with an issue before the council would of course need to recuse themselves from any and all deliberations. Its primary function would be the "judicial review" or audit function, and to resolve disputes between anchors. (See table 4.5 for descriptions of the responsibilities for each of the three anchors.)

Many schools already have Site Councils, but their roles will expand under this Democratic School Governance Model. Their work will no longer be solely relegated to subcommittee work. While this kind of work will still be an important function of council members, they will take on a more expansive leadership role, as well.

Table 4.5. Responsibilities of Anchors

Site Council and Faculty Senate	Principal	District Council
• Serve on site committees • Strategic planning • Set policies • Represent constituents • Support staff • *Faculty Senate* will also oversee curricular and assessment issues	• Manage day-to-day operations • Set and manage policies • Ensure democratic principles are followed at the building	• Highest level of grievance review • Resolve issues between anchor groups at sites • Ensure democratic principles are followed at all sites (audit function) • Judicial review

A central responsibility of Site Councils will be sharing in the establishment of the mission, vision, and values of their individual schools. Moreover, they will be responsible to frame strategic action plans (along with the principal and professional staff) corresponding to the mission, vision, and values they set.[18] Unlike the U.S. House of Representatives, however, they may not have authority over the budget, but they will certainly have influence.

Site Council members will be representative of various constituent groups. As truly democratic representatives, they will not be selected by the executive. Rather, electoral processes will need to be established whereby the various constituent groups elect their own representatives. In other words, parents will need to elect their own representatives, and faculty members will need to elect their own; these should not be appointed by the administration.

They also will appoint external representatives to the District Council. Further, underrepresented groups will need representation. It could be the role of the principal to ensure all groups are represented and the election process is fair.

The Faculty Senate will share in these responsibilities of the Site Council, but they will also be responsible for curriculum and assessment. It is imperative for us to remember that this structure provides for an equalization of power—a system of checks and balances. Additional responsibilities of the Senate and the Site Council are enumerated in the Anchor Responsibility Matrix described later in this chapter.

The principal will retain his/her authority and power through influence and daily operational responsibilities. This work would include budget development and management, staff summative evaluations, student discipline, communication with all constituent groups, and traditional leadership and bureaucratic/operational functions. In this model, the principal becomes much more of a leader than a boss. As in the higher education model, faculty will have a consultative role in these areas.

There will also be a further system of checks and balances through a newly established District Council. This council will ultimately be responsible to ensure that each anchor is functioning within its own area of responsibility and not encroaching on those of the other anchors. In other words, the council will be responsible to audit sites to ensure democratic principles and processes are being adhered. Where grievances or disputes cannot be settled at the site level, the District Council may serve as the final arbiter. We must move beyond our fear that the parents will take over our schools, and let democracy work.

It is critical to note here that most schools do not operate in a vacuum, as might be suggested in this model. Most schools are not singular entities; they reside within a district or system. Such systems have central office administrators, a superintendent, and are under the authority of a local board of education.

Any Democratic School Governance Model will need to include these two bodies in its structure. Such obligations are noted in the Anchor Responsibility Matrix to follow later in this chapter. These responsibilities are listed in an insufficient manner in the matrix, and much more detail will need to be enumerated in actual models. The Democratic School Governance Model, as suggested here, merely creates the necessary framework for ensuring democratic principles are followed and constituent groups are empowered; boards of education and central offices of administration, therefore, are not usurped in this model.

How does one begin in implementing such a Democratic School Governance Model? What should be included? How long is it going to take? This book is perhaps similar to planting a seed. Expanding on this metaphor from nature, a horticulturist would state that when transplanting a shrub, the first year it sleeps. In the second year it creeps, and in the third year it leaps. Similarly, growing and nurturing a new model will take time and will likely occur in stages.

It should be noted that schools choosing to become more democratic in practice may wish to not only focus on process and governance structures, but they might also wish to focus on curricular aspects. According to Apple and Beane, "These arrangements and opportunities [moving toward democratic governance] involve two lines of work. One is to create democratic structures and processes by which life in the school is carried out. The other is to create a curriculum that will give young people democratic experiences."[19] Democratization of the curriculum, however, is not one of the aims of this book.

In any case, as we move forward, we must always keep in mind the need to find a balance for democratic involvement with the ability to get things done in a timely fashion. Democracy is a purposefully slow, deliberative, and tedious process. Our schools, however, need to have the ability to be nimble. We cannot afford to take years in developing structures, bylaws, and proclamations. Sometimes we need to change the tire while the car is driving down the highway.

If we were to look at implementation in phases (Tier I, Tier II, and Tier III), the process and structure would be clearer and more manageable. Tier I would be the prerequisite groundwork and minimal expectations for any school considering itself to be a democratic school. This phase would most likely take a year for development and another year for initial implementation and analysis.

Tier II would represent a maturing stage of democratic development for a school as it moves toward more formalization and would require further district involvement and ownership of the model. Tier II would likely take an additional two to five years to occur. Tier III may be considered more utopian and represent a fully implemented model across the entire school district and a culture of democratic decision making. After Tier II was fully implemented, it may very well take another three to five years or more for a robust Tier III model to emerge across a school district.

TIER I

Schools and their leaders who are taking their first steps on this journey to more truly democratic processes would be considered in Tier I. It should be expected that such initial steps would take one or two years. It would seem prudent that initial implementation steps should be taken within these first two years lest people lose motivation and become frustrated in attempts to design the perfect system. Democracy is not perfect and neither will these efforts.

Initial planning will most likely begin in an informal manner. A school principal or teacher leader, for example, may begin by having informal discussions with school colleagues and maybe a few parents. If such dialogue finds some sparks of excitement and intrigue, then perhaps a formal discussion will begin. It is at such a point that the features as outlined below should be prepared in a rather detailed fashion—at least sufficiently to which people can respond and have a good idea how this model might look. An ad hoc team could frame these core ideas in a method akin to our nation's Second Continental Congress.

Identification and description of core values for democratic decision making would seem to be an appropriate starting point. For example, we learned from the Declaration of Independence that all people are created equally and that the leaders receive their power and authority from their constituents. Do we agree with these concepts in the school setting? Do we need to agree on additional concepts? We also learned that five core democratic values include liberty, common good, justice, equality, and diversity. How would we define these in our school setting? Do we agree with these? Do we need to describe them or add to them?

In chapter 3 we also learned of four constitutional principles as they relate to the workplace. These are rule of law, separation of powers, representative government, and checks and balances. Again, how would we describe these in our school setting? Are they sufficient, or do more need to be added? We also learned that the First Amendment in the Bill of Rights spoke to the necessity of freedom of speech and assembly. We need to keep this idea in mind as we frame our structures and processes.

After these core values and principles are agreed upon, the next step would focus on creating three coequal branches or anchors. Articles I, II, and III of the U.S. Constitution describe these branches (as described in chapter 3). A bicameral Site Council and Faculty Senate should be considered. In any case, responsibilities of each of these three anchors, and the roles of the Central Office and Board of Education, should be defined.

The Anchor Responsibility Matrix would be necessary to provide the appropriate focus for each group. The sample matrix included in this chapter provides a fairly comprehensive list of responsibilities. More may be added, but each will need to be defined and understood.

After such values and principles have been chosen and a general framework for the three anchors has been described by this ad hoc team, it would be necessary to gain support from senior administration at the central office if this has not already occurred earlier. Once such approval has been secured, it would be appropriate to begin listening sessions with faculty and staff and with parents.

Various listening sessions would most likely require a presentation by the committee members followed by opportunities for each constituent group to enter dialogue and ask questions. Feedback from each group would be gathered and then considered by the ad hoc committee later. This process might occur one or two more times as revisions and clarifications are made, perhaps through an affinity process.

Again, it is important that this process does not get dragged to a halt. Each model will be imperfect. However, as Winston Churchill famously stated, "Democracy is the worst form of government, except for all others." The model must not be static; rather, it must be malleable—a living structure that can grow, change, and improve over time.

Once it appears that a strong level of support exists across constituent groups, these values and beliefs, rules or bylaws, anchors and responsibilities need to be codified in writing. Perhaps rather than being called a "constitution" they can be referred to as a "compact" or similar concept. Then the constituent groups of faculty, staff, parents, and perhaps students would need to vote or ratify the agreement.

It would seem to make a great deal of sense that high school students would be considered an active constituency. Whether or to what degree middle school students and even elementary school students should be considered constituent groups would be up for debate. While they may or may not have a formal role on the Site Council, they will need to have voice in some decision-making processes. Again, these areas should be codified in writing.

From the beginning of formal discussions to ratification of the compact, one year will likely have passed. Most likely, it will take another full year of planning to put structures and processes into place. In other words, it may have taken two years in planning and developing before real implementation would begin in the third year. Again, this planning process should not take too long, as constituent motivation and energy will begin to wane.

An Anchor Responsibility Matrix (see table 4.6) such as the one presented below should be developed to help each of the three anchors, and the Central Office and Board of Education understand which areas of responsibility belong under each anchor domain. The matrix should be revisited on an annual basis, as it is likely that the degree of democratic involvement will change over time and other responsibilities will need further elaboration.

Table 4.6. Anchor Responsibility Matrix

Decisions	Site Council/ Faculty Senate	Principal	District Council	Central Office/ Board of Education
Planning				
Mission/Vision	SC4/FS4	P4		CO4/BE4
School Goals	SC4/FS4	P4		CO3/BE3
Strategic Planning	SC4/FS4	P4		CO3/BE3
Instruction				
Curriculum	FS4	P4		CO4/BE3
Assessment	FS4	P4		CO4/BE3
State/Federal Regulations				CO1
Budget				
Operational	SC3/FS3	P2		CO3
Salaries				CO1
Merit Pay		P1		
Purchasing	SC3/FS3	P2		CO3
Personnel				
Hiring	SC3/FS4	P2		CO2
Staffing	SC3/FS3	P2		
Supervision	FS4	P4		
Evaluation		P1		
Staff Development	FS2	P3		
School Committees/ Operations				
Facility Use	SC3	P2		
Scheduling	FS3	P2		
Safety Guidelines	SC3	P2		

For example, more student involvement will likely be added. Formal participation of a Student Council would be quite appropriate. Further, as building and district administration become more trusting and comfortable with this model, they may begin to yield more shared governance authority to the school anchors. For example, the Site Council might move from merely providing input into safety policies to actual shared decision making with the principal.

During the development of the three anchors, the ad hoc committee should consider how Site Council, Faculty Senate, and District Council membership is determined. Certainly for the Site Council and Faculty Senate an apportionment should be predetermined with a decision made regarding term limits.

In addition, an election process should be decided upon rather than an appointment process. This will help to assure constituents that mem-

Decisions	Site Council/ Faculty Senate	Principal	District Council	Central Office/ Board of Education
Discipline		P1		
Policies	SC4/FS4	P4		
Democratic Integrity				
Annual Review of Governance Processes			DC	
Resolve Disputes			DC	

*A simple X could be placed along the row of each item listed in the matrix under the appropriate group. In most cases, decisions/items would need varying levels of cooperation from different groups, so a more nuanced system as shown in an abbreviated form below could be developed.
P1—Principal has unilateral decision-making authority.
P2—Principal has decision-making authority with input from other groups.
P3—Principal has input.
P4—Principal shares responsibility with other group(s).
SC1—Site Council has unilateral decision-making authority.
SC2—Site Council has decision-making authority with input from principal or other groups.
SC3—Site Council has input.
SC4—Site Council shares responsibility with other group(s).
FS1—Faculty Senate has unilateral decision-making authority.
FS2—Faculty Senate has decision-making authority with input from other groups.
FS3—Faculty Senate has input.
FS4—Faculty Senate shares responsibility with other group(s).
CO1—Central Office has unilateral decision-making authority.
CO2—Central Office has decision-making authority with input from other groups.
CO3—Central Office has input.
CO4—Central Office shares responsibility with other group(s).
BE1—Board of Education has sole decision-making authority.
BE2—Board of Education has sole decision-making authority with consultation from groups.
BE3—Board of Education has input.
BE4—Board of Education shares responsibility with other group(s).
DC—District Council responsibility.

bership is fair and representative. Further, a process to ensure minority representation (understood in its broadest sense) will need to be addressed. We must learn to trust the process of democracy and fight the urge to control it.

Further, a chair of both these bicameral anchors will need to be determined. The chair of the Site Council would most likely be determined from within the Site Council itself and elected by the membership. On the other hand, the chair of the Faculty Senate could either come from within the Senate itself or the assistant principal of the school could serve in this role, much like our U.S. Senate, where the vice president serves as chair. This would also be congruent with the historical notion of the school principal (or assistant principal, in this case) serving in the role of "principal teacher."

Finally, both the principal and the Site Council/Faculty Senate should on occasion host public fora or "State of the School" sessions. Such sessions should be recorded. This is an opportunity for these anchors to share what has been accomplished over the past year or semester, and to set forth their goals for the coming year or semester.

With respect to the District Council, membership will need special consideration. Should council members be elected or appointed? The first order of business would be to determine representation. It would seem appropriate to have membership from school sites, faculty, professional staff, parents, board of education, and central office administration to likely include school building representation. Such membership could be appointed by the superintendent of the school district rather than through election, at least in the Tier I phase.

While the District Council would be charged with arbitrating grievances across anchors, its primary role would be monitoring or auditing the degree to which each anchor is adhering to the democratic principles the site or district has espoused. In other words, it would determine the degree to which each anchor is following its chartered responsibilities. In order to facilitate analysis of the degree to which individual schools and the school district adhere to the democratic principles, a Democratic Principles Matrix might be configured (see chapter 5).

In the Tier I and Tier II years, the District Council would be also responsible to monitor the change process as schools and the district move from the traditional organizational model to the new democratic schools model. This anchor group would serve as an external set of eyes to provide feedback to the individual sites and to the school district during this time of transition.

Of course, in cases where individual members have pending issues in front of the District Council, they would need to recuse themselves from discussions and deliberations. For example, if there were to be a discussion regarding Washington High School's implementation of the model, no District Council member associated with that high school would be permitted to participate.

In keeping with the spirit of the system of checks and balances embedded in our nation's democratic governance model, the Site Council and Faculty Senate would be afforded the opportunity to create amendments to site bylaws and to override principal vetoes. Conversely, the principal would have his or her own veto authority. Potentially, they could also appoint representation to the District Council.

TIER II

Tier II would most likely begin after a full year of implementation of the process has occurred. In other words, a school will need to have gone through a full year "trying on its new clothes" before it can see where it needs to make adjustments. While some schools may wish to jump in with both feet and involve students in democratic decision making, most likely many districts would prefer to wait until the Tier II stage to empower students. The Anchor Responsibility Matrix could be adjusted accordingly. A good place to begin with student involvement is the determination of responsibilities and rights of the Student Council.

An ad hoc committee, or more likely the District Council, would need to watch and assess or audit the first couple of years during this implementation stage. Prior to the implementation stage, this group would need to establish what they plan to monitor and how. For example, are people participating in each group? How were elections held for the Site Council and the Faculty Senate? Are each of the anchor groups following their own responsibilities and not encroaching on those of the other anchor groups (or following the Anchor Responsibility Matrix)? Are there open meetings and published agendas and minutes?

In addition, they would need to establish protocols for hearing complaints from one anchor against another. Whether this group is the District Council or an ad hoc team, it would need to hold at least an occasional listening session, and provide feedback and recommendations. In other words, a transparent system of checks and balances needs to be created and followed. This will be the responsibility of the District Council or ad hoc group and will be especially crucial during the formative years.

During these Tier II years, changes will invariably need to be made. The compact and bylaws, policies, and responsibility matrix will need to be more fully detailed and adjusted. For example, a process for amendments will need to be outlined, perhaps with a two-thirds vote needed by the Site Council and Faculty Senate. One full cycle for representation of Site Council and Faculty Senate members will have occurred, as well.

At the Tier II level, one or more schools may likely begin their journey into this democratic school process. In addition, the central offices would need to begin to more fully implement these concepts. Various central office divisions would likely create their own versions of responsibility matrices. For example, the offices of Human Resources, Curriculum and Assessment, Student Services, Instructional Services, Institutional Technology, and the like would need to adapt their own matrix versions to those used by the school sites.

Further, just as Article IV of the U.S. Constitution addresses issues related to how various states interact and their rights, so too should school districts consider how various schools, both newly democratically organized and their traditional counterparts, interact with one another and the school district in the degree to which they have autonomy and common rules, regulations, policies, and processes.

TIER III

Tier III will be reserved for matured organizations. This would result from a full-fledged district governance model where all schools are mature in their development, policies and practices are fully implemented, and democratic governance and decision making is fully a part of the district culture and each site. Chapter 5 will be devoted to a final discussion encompassing Tier III organizations.

SAM WANTS YOU

Stuff was getting real now for Sam. She met with her professional colleagues and with the Student Council. It had helped tremendously to have her ideas formulated with a framework and displayed on the Prezi. It made a difference by focusing everyone's attention and not going astray with extraneous questions. In fact, Sam was very pleased with the feedback she received from her faculty and staff members with whom she met. There was unanimous agreement that this concept was worth pursuing. Teachers Gene Jones and Greta McGovern agreed to assist Sam as she met with the Student Council and Jose Perez.

Even the meeting with the Student Council went better than Sam had anticipated. Willis Davidson and the officers of the council were very pleased that their idea was on their principal's agenda and that she actually took time to prepare the Prezi with sufficient detail to show that she was serious. Even more, it meant a lot to them that two of their teachers helped to make the presentation.

While the vast majority of the eleven Student Council members were in favor of continuing the discussion, a couple seemed nonplussed, and one showed signs of skepticism. While the overall reception of the council was in agreement to move forward, the students echoed comments of the faculty; they were concerned that Washington High School would not get approval to go ahead with this new model. It was clear to Sam she now needed to meet with her boss.

While seated outside Superintendent Carleson's office, Samantha felt uneasy. She was confident in her abilities and her ideas, but she was not confident in the reception she would receive. Through the class partition to his office window, Samantha could see Dr. Carleson and associate superintendent Bernice Pelligrini talking with one another; they even glanced her way a couple of times during their conversation. Finally, Dr. Carleson summoned Samantha to his office. "Thank you for meeting with me, Michael and Bernice," Samantha started.

"We're happy to talk with you, Sam. As you know, we're very proud of our School District of Distinction national recognition. I think we're an excellent model of shared decision making, don't you?" asked Dr. Carleson.

"Of course," Sam responded.

Hardly waiting for her response, Bernice interjected, "In order to be selected as a School District of Distinction, we had to provide evidence that shared decision making is an integral part of our culture. Each school needs a Site Council or PTO, budgets must be transparent, and the student standardized test scores must be better than the state average in the aggregate. We've held this distinction three years running."

"Of course," Sam again responded, feeling a sense of rejection before she even had her chance to speak.

Dr. Carleson continued. "In that vein of forward thinking, I am anxious to listen to your thoughts, Samantha."

With just a bit of trepidation, Sam handed a copy of the notes for her Prezi presentation to both of her superiors. She decided to jump right in. She covered her presentation just as she did with her teachers and staff; however, she caught herself talking a bit faster this time. On one occasion, Dr. Carleson gently put his hand on Bernice's arm as she was about to say something. It took a good twenty minutes of Sam speaking alone. She finished and asked, "Those are my thoughts; any questions? Oh, I have spoken with a small group of teachers at Washington, and the Student Council asked to speak with me about this. See, they helped push me along after our trip to the capital. With your permission, I would like to present to the parents."

Dr. Carleson turned his head to the side and rested his chin on his knuckles. A small smile crossed his face as he closed his eyes. Both Bernice and Samantha stared at him. He paused for several long moments. Bernice was hoping for a smackdown, and Samantha was hoping for carte blanche approval to move ahead on her own. Neither was to be the case.

"Sam, you've got me interested. This makes me think of a charter school—a place that we can experiment on the side without impacting the entire district." The superintendent continued, "Before we get parents involved, I want you to join me over lunch tomorrow with Board President Phylford. It's our weekly lunch meeting. Please bring along a couple more copies of your handout."

Samantha nodded in agreement and said, "I'll clear my calendar." With that, both she and Bernice walked out together in silence—neither looking at the other. Stuff was getting real.

The lunch was held at Len Phylford's executive suite, where he enjoyed the privileges as CEO of one of the local IT firms. In fact, it was the same firm that recently hired Gene Jones's wife. The first half hour of the conversation seemed odd and at times uncomfortable to Samantha. Michael and Len were discussing things that she had not been privy to in the past. She felt like a fly on the wall as her boss discussed possible changes in arbitration laws and how that would impact teacher contract negotiations, and as Len talked about the future need (in the very near term) for a new school complex. With the rebound in the economy and an impressive influx of young millennials looking for employment in the IT sector, this would need to be addressed sooner than later.

They were eating dessert by the time Dr. Carleson asked Samantha to share her idea. He let her do all the talking with only minor interjections along the way. He looked both excited and proud. While Sam was concerned yesterday about turning her site into a charter school, Dr. Carleson presented this as a viable option. Len loved the entire idea, but he was concerned about the charter idea, but for reasons different than those of Samantha. He felt all schools would deserve this right and there would be friction between teachers and parents of the two other high schools. In the end, the idea of a charter seemed wisest, as it would allow the district the opportunity to work out the bugs.

As they got up to leave, Samantha had some mixed feelings. For the most part, she was excited that she was given approval to move ahead. There was a lingering feeling, however, that she might be losing ownership. Would central office begin to take control?

At the Washington School Parent Council (WSPC) meeting, Principal Levy was joined by Gene Jones, Greta McGovern, and students Willis Davidson and Elizabeth Van Dyke. It was interesting to see two onlookers in the audience—Gene Jones's wife and Bernice Pelligrini.

This time, Samantha started the Prezi presentation, but the bulk of the talking was by this ad hoc group. The two students led the question-and-answer period. Samantha was more than a little dismayed at the lack of questions and enthusiasm from the parents. After all, it would seem that they would have the greatest desire to become more involved in their children's school. While there was no real animosity in the discussion with the parents, Samantha felt a sense of apathy. One parent stated that he didn't have time to be involved in a way that would be necessary or productive. A few other heads nodded; some folks held their arms crossed against their chests.

A flicker of hope ignited for Samantha when the parent council cochair Jane Archer and council member Veronica Villereal agreed to serve on an ad hoc committee with the charge of developing this model and with communicating with all constituent groups.

KEY POINTS

- The more freedom and power people have in decision making, the more responsibility they have with it.

- Sustained and substantive change initiates at the lower levels of an organization.
- Emergent structures are ways to make bureaucracies more responsive to the need for change.
- Three conditions are necessary for shared governance models: (1) a structure that encourages wide participation and relationships across the systems; (2) a structure that is flexible in terms of supporting communication both laterally and horizontally in the organization; and (3) a structure that empowers constituents but at the same time holds them accountable.
- The Higher Education Shared Governance Model can serve as an aspirant example for local schools.

POINTS TO PONDER

1. What are some useful ideas you can use from the Higher Education Shared Governance Model?
2. What are the faculty and the administration responsibilities in the Higher Education Shared Governance Model?
3. Describe in some detail the responsibilities of the three anchors in a Democratic School Governance Model.
4. How are the roles of the principal, teachers and staff, and parents different than those in the current structure at your school?
5. What should be the roles of the Central Office and the Board of Education in a Democratic School Governance Model?

NOTES

1. Archon Fung and Erik Olin Wright, eds., *Deepening Democracy: Institutional Innovations in Empowered Participatory Governance* (London: Verso, 2003), 25.

2. Edward S. Greenberg, *Workplace Democracy: The Political Effects of Participation* (New York: Cornell University Press, 1986), 50.

3. Ibid, 43.

4. Robert Jackall and Joyce Crain, "The Contemporary Small Cooperative Movement," Robert Jackall and Henry M. Levin, eds., *Worker Cooperatives in America* (Berkeley, CA: University of California Press, 1984), 96.

5. Paulo Freire, *Pedagogy of the Oppressed* (New York: Continuum, 1970).

6. Howard Zinn, *Declarations of Independence: Cross-Examining American Ideology* (New York: Harper Perennial, 1990), 178–79.

7. Teresa M. Harrison, "Designing the Post-Bureaucratic Organization: New Perspectives on Organizational Change" (*Australian Journal of Communication* 1992) 19, 24. Harrison further stipulates, "The new experiments involve more participative approaches to the design and execution of work, decentralized decision making processes requiring greater levels of employee involvement and a general de-emphasis on managerial authority, and the elimination of levels of structure—all significant infringements on the traditional features of bureaucratic hierarchy" (22).

8. Perry R. Rettig, "Beyond Organizational Tinkering: A New View of School Reform," *Educational Horizons* (Summer 2004): 264.

9. Charles Heckscher, "Defining the Post-Bureaucratic Type," Charles Heckscher and Anne Donnellon, eds., *The Post-Bureaucratic Organization: New Perspectives on Organizational Change* (Thousand Oaks, CA: Sage, 1994), 39–41. Heckscher goes on to explain three distinct advantages to using such interactive structures. "The most important strength is that decisions result from a thorough 'mixing' of the intelligence found throughout the organization. . . . The second major advantage is . . . interactive structures create a framework for greater responsiveness to environmental changes. . . . Closely related to these points is the probability that an interactive structure is better for the creation of evolutionary new forms" (50–51).

10. Ibid., 41

11. Francis X. Neumann Jr., "Organizational Structures to Match the New Information-Rich Environments: Lessons from the Study of Chaos," *Public Productivity and Management Review* (September 1997): 96.

12. William E. Halal, *The New Management: Bringing Management and Markets Inside Organizations* (San Francisco: Berrett-Koehler, 1998), 30. Halal explained how these new systems work. It means that the locus of control will move out of the hands of the top executives so that it can be shared by operating managers, workers, clients, and others who are involved. An organic organization can be under far more *effective* (emphasis in original) control because decisions are made throughout the system by people close to the action. The strength of an organic system is that it is more sensitive to the need for change because control is exercised constantly all about in response to the ebb and flow of environmental forces. People ordinarily resist change, not because they are obstinate, but because they are fearful when change is forced on them. If change originates *from* (emphasis in original) them, however, they can

accept it because they are in control of their lives. Many thrive on self-created change because it gives them a sense of mastery over their future (197).

13. Fritjof Capra, *The Hidden Connections: A Science for Sustainable Living* (New York: Anchor Books, 2004), 121.

14. Archon Fung, *Empowered Participation: Reinventing Urban Democracy* (Princeton, NJ: Princeton University Press, 2004), 224. This is an excellent book that describes, in detail, not only the accountable-autonomy model, but also the transformative work of the CPS and the CPD. "In 1998, the Illinois legislature enacted school-reform legislation for Chicago that broke apart the CPS into a decentralized, participatory system. The law devolved control of many aspects of school operation to parents and local staff, it opened operations to popular participation, and problem-solving became the core task of these school governments" (39–40). In addition, some of the local Site Councils hire, evaluate, and renew/nonrenew their school administrators.

15. Patrick Dolan, *Restructuring Our Schools: A Primer on Systemic Change* (Kansas City, MO: Systems and Organizations), 1994.

16. "Constitutional Topic: Checks and Balances," 2005, pgs. 1–2. URL: http://usconstitution.net/consttop_cnb.html.

17. William G. Bowen and Eugene M. Tobin, *Locus of Authority: The Evolution of Faculty Roles in Governance of Higher Education* (Princeton, NJ: Princeton University Press and ITHACA, 2015), 93–94. [The author of this book has served as a K–12 teacher and principal, and as a college faculty member and vice president. It is his experience that higher education provides far greater professional autonomy and decision-making responsibility for faculty than is provided to K–12 teachers. School principals clearly exert their power through their legal authority, while college deans, vice presidents, and presidents exert their influence with the budget and through the art of persuasion. This model would serve as a productive aspirant model for K–12 schools.]

18. Perry R. Rettig and Dale Feinauer, "Rethinking the Role and Function of School Site Councils," *Wisconsin School News* (June 2002): 12–13. This article describes the three primary purposes of school Site Councils, as well as areas for which they are not designed.

19. Michael W. Apple and James A. Beane, eds., *Democratic Schools, Second Edition: Lessons in Powerful Education* (Heinemann Publishing, 2007), 9–10. This book and others described in the bibliography provide fine detail into democratic curriculum whereby students have an important voice in what and how they learn. Such a focus on student empowerment in curricular decision making, however, is not a focus of this book.

CHAPTER 5

Back to the Future

This journey of a thousand miles begins with a single step. Let us begin by talking about talking. Democratic decision-making processes and dialogue are requisite central features to any school system that chooses to provide a critical praxis and dialectic as defined by Paulo Freire.[1] Critical dialogue is the vehicle for practitioners to become aware of their condition, their promise, and the path to get there.[2] "The issue raised for organizational communication scholars is how to design a structure that integrates wider participation and provides for the expertise required for effective decision making."[3]

Viviane Robinson elucidated as to how this is to be done:

> Participants in a problem-solving discourse must be committed to three discourse values. The first, that of respect, ensures ... fair opportunity to speak, to challenge or to continue any line of inquiry, to express one's feeling and to be in general unconstrained in one's dealing with the other parties in the discourse. The second discourse value is that of commitment to valid information. It involves commitment to the conduct of discourse in ways that increase the chances of detection of error in one's own and others' claims about the nature of the problem and how to solve it ... they welcome rather than discourage different perspectives.... The third value, that of commitment to the process and outcomes of dialogue ... involves being motivated to expend the intellectual and emotional effort required until all parties can proclaim to each other and to third parties that they have a solution that is the best they can construct, given their mutually agreed constraints on the problems.[4]

Therefore, it will be critical for democratic school leaders to create opportunities for teachers and staff, fellow administrators, students and their parents, and community members to begin dialogue about their values, their participatory roles and commensurate responsibilities, and the way forward. Most likely such dialogue will begin informally, but more formal and structured opportunity for such interaction will need to occur rather quickly.

Such conversations will not be of a one-time nature, but this will necessitate an iterative process and opportunities to bring diverse groups together to share in the dialogue. Indeed, running such interactions will demand different types of skills of our emerging democratic leaders. These individuals will need to "give strong leadership. Not strong in the sense of authority, but in terms of strength of purpose, of holding to your democratic values even when things get difficult. Tenacity and humility in a leader call for greater strength of character than the exercise of power," according to Backman and Trafford.[5]

Teachers and their students must also use critical dialogue in their classrooms. As it stands in our contemporary classrooms across the country, students—in reality—are treated as passive sponges soaking up knowledge. They have very little say in where they are placed, what they learn, how they learn, and how their progress is to be evaluated.

Paulo Freire noted, "The more students work at storing the deposits entrusted to them, the less they develop the critical consciousness which would result from their intervention in the world as transformers of that world. The more completely they accept the passive role imposed on them, the more they tend simply to adapt to the world as it is and to the fragmented view of reality deposited in them."[6]

Specifically, what are teachers to do? Beyer and Bigelow give us some insight. "Effective teachers reflect critically on the moral, political, social, and economic dimensions of education. This requires an understanding of the multiple contexts in which schools function, an appreciation of diverse perspectives on educational issues, and a commitment to democratic forms of interaction." Furthermore, "One function of the school curriculum is to celebrate the culture of the dominate and to ignore or scorn the culture of the subordinate groups. . . . Students . . . can *create* [emphasis in original] knowledge, not simply absorb it from higher authorities."[7]

William Bigelow went on to state, "I do not think that our classrooms can ever be exact models of the kind of participatory democracy we would like to have characterize the larger society. If teachers' only power were to grade students, that would be sufficient to sabotage classroom democracy. However, classrooms can offer students experiences and understandings that counter, and critique, the lack of democracy in the rest of their lives. In the character of student interactions the classroom can offer a glimpse of certain features of an egalitarian society."[8]

With that said, Tier III will demand a focus on the students unlike that which has been described in Tiers I and II. Students' voices will need to be heard as they begin to take more ownership and responsibility for their own education. "A democratic curriculum invites young people to shed the passive role of knowledge consumers and assume the active role of 'meaning makers.'"[9]

This does not mean that each student votes on the curriculum and other various aspects of their education, but they should have a voice; they should somehow, somewhere have a seat at the table. Not only do they need a voice, but they need to become responsible for their education.

Roles of students will not be the only ones that need to be examined and to change. Clearly, the role of the executive, the school leadership, will necessarily see significant change. Present governance models have the executive deriving their power from their positional authority. A democratic model will shift the primary focus of power from one derived through formal position to more the individual's ability to relate, to empower the process and the constituent groups, to persuade—to truly lead.

It would then seem that the assistant principalship is an excellent training ground for democratic leadership. The position has little traditional power other than that it receives from positional authority. The new assistant principal will gain power via the art of persuasion—persuasion of the principal and over the faculty senate. This is an opportunity to regain the historic role of "principal teacher."

Teachers and staff will need to modify their roles, as well. They will need time to deliberate and participate in the governance process; work schedules may need adjustment. Parents and school board members will see a change in their relationships to school personnel in order to create this requisite time. Parents will be an integral part of leadership and need to consider all points of view other than just what appears to be in the best interest of their own children.

School board members will need to be mindful of process, to make certain that democratic principles are being followed across the district and slippage back into the old order does not occur. In order to make sound decisions, these newly involved groups will need information—information that has traditionally only been under the purview of administration. They will also need to understand that with these new freedoms come new responsibilities in terms of the time commitment, to the democratic values of shared decision making, and to the very processes of democratic decision making.

It should also be reiterated that democratic decision-making processes don't require people or groups to vote on everything. Quite often all that is truly necessary is the opportunity to share in discussion, have information available, and to have decisions made in a transparent fashion.

Natsiopoulou and Giouroukakis discuss the concept of democratic and distributed school leadership as it exists in Ellinikon, Greece. Here, all faculty are contractually required to participate in the Teacher Assembly and participate in the administration of the school.[10] This approach closely resembles the roles of teachers in democratic schools as espoused in this book.

It is the concept of auditing that will be so necessary as schools and school districts move into democratic maturity. The District Council should be charged with this responsibility of "judicial review." "Ultimately, each presumed case of workplace democratization needs careful scrutiny with respect to such dimensions as (a) the range of issues about which participants may speak, (b) the extent of actual influence by employees through their exercise of voice, and (c) the levels of the hierarchy at which meaningful voice is possible."[11]

It would appear that these fundamental beliefs have as their core tenets the belief in honesty, openness, and fairness. Workers must be treated fairly, open communication and decision making is essential, and processes must be transparent. As a school district moves to inclusion of all school sites as democratic entities, it will need to further consider centralization versus decentralization or some manner of the concept of federalism. The District Council will need to make certain those who are newly empowered in this model don't become too powerful—or that "the oppressed become the oppressors." A Democratic Principles Matrix (see table 5.1) such as the one that follows might be created to help focus the District Council's work.

A final note of interest should be made here. From a review of the literature, there are sporadic examples of democratic schools throughout the United States. These are usually isolated to individual private or charter schools, and their practices involve students thoroughly in self-determination of their learning and in school governance. Often their rights are equivalent to those of faculty. Still, these examples are isolated and don't appear to be widespread throughout an entire school district.[12]

Of further interest is the democratic school movement in Europe. The European Democratic Schools movement as described by Backman and Trafford bears investigation.[13] These authors describe the work of the Council of Europe as it pertains to the Three Principles for Education for Democratic Citizenship. The principles are rights and responsibilities, active participation, and valuing diversity.

Some final thoughts as we begin this journey are appropriate here. All groups involved in a shift to democratic governance will need to be mindful of the lessons learned in chapter 3 about the process of change. Most notably, it will take time—time to develop and the precious time of participation—and patience. Such a human endeavor, a culture shift, will not go smoothly. Those who feel they will be losing power will fight change the fiercest. Likewise, this endeavor must not be seen as

Table 5.1. Democratic Principles Matrix

Principle	Meets Expectations	Making Good Progress	Needs Improvement
Checks/balances			
Separation of power			
Representation			
Communication			
Transparency			
*Comments:			

a form of manipulation by the administration—"the iron fist wrapped in a velvet glove."

The mindset of shared decision making and democratic processes will require training for all constituent groups. Support from both administration and all constituent groups is necessary. An Anchor Responsibility Matrix and a Democratic Principles Matrix will need to be developed and agreed upon by all groups. A new culture must become institutionalized in order to be sustainable, and someone or some group must be responsible to keep making progress—that one initial champion to keep everyone focused and on track.

In the now famous words of Martin Luther as he took on the authorities of the church, "Here I stand; I can do no other."

HIT THE ROAD, SAM

Samantha attended a peace rally that evening at the high school. There continued to be growing strife in the community. Local civic and church leaders invited Reverend Jesse Jackson to attend and speak to a community that was becoming increasingly disenfranchised with government institutions—city hall, the police, the schools.[14]

After nearly an hour of short speeches by the mayor, state congressman Doyle, and local pastors, a student from a city parochial school introduced the Reverend Jesse Jackson. He emerged from behind the auditorium's screened stage. The crowd rose to its feet in a thunderous applause.

After thanking those in attendance, Reverend Jackson began his metronome-like ticking off of social malaise and youthful angst, middle-class dystopia, and worker pay inequities. The energy in the auditorium was growing, and then the preacher took a deep breath and a prolonged pause as he looked at the dignitaries seated behind him on the stage. Then he turned to the audience for his final comments.

"Friends, every day people tell me they have no power. They can't make a difference; they can't change the system. But I tell them they are wrong. They may not have *formal authority* in their places of employment or in their government, but they have *power*! You all have power!"

After a number of cheers, applause, and Amens, Reverend Jackson continued. "Folks, you have the power of your values, of your beliefs, of your convictions. You have the power of each other! Never for a moment think that you don't have power. Indeed, in our history power has only come from the people. There is more power in this room right now than in any office in the city, in your state, or in your nation." With that, Reverend Jackson left the stage and walked down the side aisle shaking hands with those in attendance. Samantha Levy's was the third hand he shook; it was a moment she would never forget.

When Sam and the ad hoc team met with the faculty, Jose reminded everyone that they all needed to keep in mind that democracy is a purposefully slow and tedious process. It is designed to be deliberative so that decisions aren't made too quickly without a great deal of thought and input. Sam countered that our schools, however, need to have the ability to remain nimble in order to be responsive in a timely fashion. In other words, we need to find a balance for democratic involvement with the ability to get things done. Clearly, the team had their act together. But from the response from the faculty, it was clear that a great deal of discussion had happened behind the scenes—the idea of this new model had been leaked. And it seemed more than a bit strange that Bernice Pelligrini was back in attendance.

The first faculty member to speak up was Dr. Howard Pranceton—the elder statesman of the school and chair of the Mathematics Department. "Ms. Levy, through my tenure at Washington High School, I have seen many principals come and go—all with their ideas for change and improvement. Over that time, I have seen our school move from the only high school to one of three in the district. We have had some very difficult times and some very good times. Presently, we are experiencing a period of academic excellence even with financial difficulties. Such a change that you are thinking of seems to be unnecessary."

Chemistry teacher Norm Schimansky echoed those sentiments. "That's right! We're not broken! Why fix something that isn't broken?"

Kathleen Parson, veteran French teacher, agreed. "We are an extremely busy and service-oriented faculty. We are committed to quality education for our students, and it shows. I don't understand why you want to change this. I don't have time to reinvent this wheel."

Music teacher Priscilla Proponov followed: "In yesterday's class I was interrupted by one of my students. He said he didn't have to do the homework assigned because soon he would be my boss. He said, 'Majority rules!'"

Jose quickly stood up. "That was a totally inappropriate comment. We are suggesting no such thing here."

Willis Davidson joined Jose. "I'm sorry that happened, Ms. Proponov. That was a stupid statement by a stupid student. What I am requesting is that Washington High School teachers, the principal, students, and parents put together a system that is more like the ideals we learn from our U.S. history classes. We learn about democracy in textbooks and in class, but we don't see it here. I assure you, we are taking this seriously. All that I ask is that you take us just as seriously."

Several comments, pro and con, continued over the next fifteen minutes. But the initial heat appeared to have been taken out of the meeting. Samantha glanced at Bernice Pelligrini. She had been taking notes during the debate, which had now come to a close. Finally, she got up and walked out of the auditorium, talking earnestly with a small group of teachers.

Before Samantha arrived for work the next morning, she received a text message from Dr. Carleson. He wanted to see her before she went to Washington High.

As she entered his office, Samantha could tell something was wrong. Dr. Carleson looked rather pale as he motioned her to sit in front of his desk.

"Samantha, I think you've taken this democratic idea too literally and too quickly. Bernice tells me that after your faculty session yesterday afternoon a group of your teachers met with her. Samantha, your faculty will be holding a 'no-confidence vote' about your leadership."

Samantha sat stunned, her eyes wide open. "What do you mean, Dr. Carleson?"

Michael Carleson got up from behind his desk and began to pace in front of his window overlooking the river below. "There are a number of professionals at Washington High School who don't understand your plans or why you're doing this. They feel this is going to blow up on them right away, and that the kids are going to be running the school. I was told that you met with parents before you met with the faculty. They want to know what this young principal is up to, and they want to know what I'm going to do about it!"

"I'm sorry, Dr. Carleson. I didn't know they were so upset. I mean, I knew there were some concerns, but nothing that seemed couldn't be understood or rectified."

They both sat in silence for a few moments. Then Samantha continued. "We have so many people excited about this idea, and we've had broad participation. Who wants to vote no-confidence?"

"Well, Samantha," Superintendent Carleson bounced back. "Knowing who wants such a vote would seem undemocratic." The sting was apparent on Samantha's face. Dr. Carleson continued. "Furthermore, you mentioned you have broad participation. How many faculty members have been involved?"

After a few minutes of this exchange, Dr. Carleson concluded, "Sam, I'm going to have to meet with your faculty and listen to them. Please schedule a full faculty meeting for 3:30 this afternoon in your auditorium." With that, Sam exited her boss's office; her eyes began to fill with tears, so she quickened her pace. As she opened the suite door, Bernice walked in. Nothing was said. Samantha's mind bolted to the speech given by Reverend Jackson; she felt entirely powerless. Even worse, she was afraid for her job.

KEY POINTS

- There are three problem-solving discourse values: (1) respect (fair opportunity to speak); (2) a commitment to valid information; and (3) a commitment to the process and outcomes of dialogue.
- A "critical dialogue" is necessary for teachers if they would choose to embrace a democratic classroom.
- A Democratic Principles Matrix needs to be created in order to provide an auditing function of each of the anchors.

POINTS TO PONDER

1. What would the three problem-solving discourse values look like in practice at your school?
2. What would critical dialogue look like in your classrooms?
3. Edit and expand on the Democratic Principles Matrix.
4. How do you begin the Tier I dialogue? With whom will you speak? What are the concepts and questions you will discuss?

NOTES

1. Paulo Freire, *Pedagogy of the Oppressed* (New York: Continuum), 1970.
2. Cheney et al., "Democracy, Participation, and Communication at Work: A Multidisciplinary Review," *Communication Yearbook* 21 (2004): 72–73. George Cheney et al. pronounced, "We must remain mindful of the postmodern critique that calls into question the very meanings of consensus and the open expression of interests. We should not take adversarial or unitary models of democratic participation for granted; rather, we ought to 'deconstruct' each type to reveal the ways in which its operation in practice may undermine its own presumed goals. This is important because most of our models of democratic participation, whether consensus-based or adversarial in orientation, presume that training and engagement in rational discussion represent progressive movement toward democratic ideals."
3. Teresa M. Harrison, "Designing the Post-Bureaucratic Organization: New Perspectives on Organizational Change," *Australian Journal of Communication* 19 (1992): 24.
4. Viviane Robinson, "Critical Theory and the Social Psychology of Change," in Keith Leithwood, ed., *International Handbook of Educational Leadership and Administration* (1996): 1085–1986.
5. Elisabeth Backman and Bernard Trafford, *Democratic Governance of Schools* (Council of Europe Publishing, 2007), 78. These authors continue, "it may be [the democratic leader's] job to ensure that there is a balance of opinion within the group and that good practice is observed: in other words, that minorities are represented. . . ." 82.
6. Ibid., Freire, 73. In a concurring opinion, Sirotnik explained, "In summarizing empirical research on 'the modal classroom,' Sirotnik concludes, 'We are implicitly teaching dependence upon authority, linear thinking, social apathy, passive involvement, and hands-off learning,' all in a 'virtually affectless environment.'" K. Sirotnik, "What You See Is What You Get: Consistency, Persistency, and Mediocrity in Classrooms," *Harvard Education Review* 53

(1983): 29 cited in L. Beyer, "The Value of Critical Perspectives in Teacher Education," *Journal of Teacher Education* 52 (March/April 2001): 155.

7. L. Beyer, "The Value of Critical Perspectives in Teacher Education," *Journal of Teacher Education* 52 (March/April 2001): 161.

8. William Bigelow, "Inside the Classroom: Social Vision and Critical Pedagogy" *Teachers College Record* 91, Columbia University: Teachers College (Spring 1990): 445. On a side note, it is my personal belief that neither students nor parents should be "evaluating" teachers or principals. It remains my belief that principals evaluate teachers and superintendents evaluate principals. However, it is quite appropriate, and even necessary, for students and parents to be provided the opportunity to provide feedback into these evaluations.

9. Michael W. Apple and James A. Beane, "The Case for Democratic Schools," in Bean and Apple, eds., *Democratic Schools* (ASCD, Alexandria, VA: 1995), 16.

10. Eleni Natsiopoulou and Vicky Giouroukakis, "When Teachers Run the School," *Educational Leadership* (April 2010): 67.

11. University of Wisconsin Center for Cooperatives, "The Microprocess Features of Workplace Democratization," *Democracy, Participation, and Communication at Work*, p. 3. www.uwcc.wisc.edu/info/democ2.html.

12. Ibid., Apple and Beane. Other books describing small-scale democratic schools include the following: Sam Chaltain, *American Schools: The Art of Creating a Democratic Learning Community* (Lanham, MD: Rowman & Littlefield Education, 2009). Michael Fielding, *Radical Education and the Common School: A Democratic Alternative* (Routledge, 2011). Matthew Knoester, *Democratic Education in Practice: Inside the Mission High School* (Teaches College Press, 2012). Eleni Natsiopoulou and Vicky Giouroukakis, "When Teachers Run the School," *Educational Leadership* (April 2010.

13. Ibid., Backman and Trafford, http://www.coe.int/edc/en. The authors consider this document a "toolkit" for schools looking to become democratic in their practices. This toolkit describes the Three Principles for Education for Democratic Citizenship (rights and responsibilities, active participation, and valuing diversity), and the Council of Europe's four Key Areas: governance, leadership, and public accountability; value-centered education; cooperation, communication, and involvement—competitiveness and school self-determination; and student discipline. The toolkit also provides a planning grid with these dimensions in relation to stages of democratic maturity. Finally, the article shares numerous examples of what they describe as democratic schools from various European nations.

14. This event and speech are both fictional. Any resemblance to actual events or speeches given by the Reverend Jesse Jackson is purely coincidental.

Bibliography

Apple, Michael W. and James A. Beane. "The Case for Democratic Schools." In *Democratic Schools,* edited by Michael Apple and James Beane, 1–29. Alexandria, VA: ASCD, 1995.

Apple, Michael W. and James A. Beane, eds. *Democratic Schools, Second Edition: Lessons in Powerful Education.* Heinemann Publishing, 2007.

Atkinson, Anthony. "The Promise of Employee Involvement." *CMA Magazine* (April 1990): 8.

Bachrach, Peter and Aryeh Botwinick. *Power and Empowerment: A Radical Theory of Participatory Democracy.* Philadelphia: Temple University Press, 1992.

Backman, Elisabeth and Bernard Trafford. "Democratic Governance of Schools." *Council of Europe Publishing* (2007): http://www.coe.int/edc/en.

Beyer, L. "The Value of Critical Perspectives in Teacher Education." *Journal of Teacher Education* 52 (March/April 2001): 151–63.

Bigelow, William. "Inside the Classroom: Social Vision and Critical Pedagogy." *Teachers College Record* 91. Columbia University: Teachers College (Spring 1990): 437–48.

Blau, P. M. *The Organization of Academic Work.* New York: Wiley, 1973.

Block, Peter. *Stewardship: Choosing Service over Self-Interest.* San Francisco: Berrett-Koehler, 1996.

Bowen, William G. and Eugene M. Tobin. *Locus of Authority: The Evolution of Faculty Roles in Governance of Higher Education.* Princeton, NJ: Princeton University Press and ITHACA, 2015.

Bransford, J., A. Brown, and A. Cocking, eds. *How People Learn: Brain, Mind, Experience, and School.* Washington, DC: National Academy Press, 1999.

Brody, David. "The Breakdown of Labor's Social Contract: Historical Reflections, Future Prospects." *Dissent* 40 (Winter 1992): 32–41.

Capra, Fritjof. *The Hidden Connections: A Science of Sustainable Living.* New York: Anchor Books, 2004.

Capra, Fritjof. *The Web of Life: A New Scientific Understanding of Living Systems.* New York: Anchor Books Doubleday, 1996.

Chaltain, Sam. *American Schools: The Art of Creating a Democratic Learning Community.* Rowman & Littlefield Education, 2009.

Cheney, George. "Democracy, Participation, and Communication at Work: A Multidisciplinary Review." In *Communication Yearbook* 21 (2004): 64.

CIVITAS. "A Framework for Civic Engagement," *A collaborative project with The Center for Civic Engagement and the Council for the Advancement of Citizenship for Civic Education and the Council for the Advancement of Citizenship, National Council for the Social Studies Bulletin,* 86, 1991. www.constitutioncenter.org/explore/TheUS.Constitution/index.shtml.

Clarke, John H. "Growing High School Reform: Planting the Seeds of Systemic Change." *NASSP Bulletin* 1 (April 1999): 1–9.

Cleaver, Eldridge. *Soul on Ice.* New York: Dell, 1968.

Chomsky, Noam. *Chomsky: On Miseducation.* Lanham, MD: Rowman & Littlefield, 2000.

Comstock, D. "A Method for Critical Research." In *Knowledge and Values in Social and Educational Research,* edited by E. Bredo and W. Feinberg. Philadelphia: Temple University Press. 1982.

Constitution Center at www.constitutioncenter.org.

"Constitutional Topic: Checks and Balances," 2005. URL: http://usconstitution.net/consttop_cnb.html.

Crandall, D. *A Study of Dissemination Efforts Supporting School Improvement.* Andover, MA: The Network, Inc., 1982.

Csikszentmihalyi, Mihaly. *Flow: The Psychology of Optimal Experience.* New York: Harper Collins, 1990.

Darling-Hammond, Linda. "Target Time Toward Teachers." *Journal of Staff Development* 20 (Spring 1999): 31–36.

Davis, E. and Russell Lansbury. *Democracy and Control in the Workplace.* Melbourne, Australia: Longman Cheshire, 1986.

Derber, Milton. *The American Idea of Democracy.* Chicago: University of Chicago Press, 1970.

Dewey, John. *Democracy and Education.* Carbondale, IL: Southern Illinois University, 2008.

DeWitt, S. *Worker Participation and the Crisis of Liberal Democracy.* Boulder, CO: Westview Press, 1980.

Diamond, Larry. https://web.stanford.edu/~ldiamond/iraq/DemocracyEducation0204.htm.

Dolan, Patrick. *Restructuring Our Schools: A Primer on Systemic Change.* Kansas City, MO: Systems and Organizations, 1994.

Donnellon, Anne and Maureen Scully. "Teams, Performance, and Rewards: Will the Post-Bureaucratic Organization be a Post-Meritocratic Organization?" In *The Post-Bureaucratic Organization: New Perspectives on Organizational Change,* edited by Charles Heckscher and Lynda Applegate, 64–78. Thousand Oaks, CA: Sage, 1994.

Dotlich, D. and P. Cairo. *Unnatural Leadership: Going Against Intuition and Experience to Develop Ten New Leadership Instincts.* San Francisco: Jossey-Bass, 2002.

European Democratic Education Community at www.eudec.com.

Fielding, Michael. *Radical Education and the Common School: A Democratic Alternative.* New York: Routledge, 2011.

Freire, Paulo. *Pedagogy of the Oppressed.* New York: Continuum, 1970.

Fung, Archon. *Empowered Participation: Reinventing Urban Democracy.* Princeton, NJ: Princeton University Press, 2004.

Fung, Archon and Erik Olin Wright, eds. *Deepening Democracy: Institutional Innovations in Empowered Participatory Governance.* London, England: Verso, 2003.

Gamson, Zelda F. and Henry M. Levin. "Obstacles to the Survival of Democratic Workplaces." In *Worker Cooperatives in America,* edited by Robert Jackall and Henry M Levin, 219–37. Berkeley, CA: University of California Press, 1984.

Gelatt, H. "Chaos and Compassion." *Counseling and Values* (January 1995): 39.

Gordon, Frederick. "Bureaucracy: Can We Do Better? Can We Do Worse?" In *The Post-Bureaucratic Organization: New Perspectives on Organizational Change,* edited by Charles Heckscher and Anne Donnellon, 195–220. Thousand Oaks, CA: Sage, 1994.

Gorton, Richard. *School Leadership and Administration: Important Concepts, Case Studies, and Simulations.* Dubuque, IA: William C. Brown, 1987.

Green, R. L. *Practicing the Art of Leadership: A Problem-Based Approach to Implementing the ISLLC Standards.* Upper Saddle River, NJ: Merrill Prentice Hall, 2001.

Greenberg, Edward. *Workplace Democracy: The Political Effects of Participation.* Ithaca, NY: Cornell University Press, 1986.

Halal, William E. *The New Management: Bringing Democracy and Markets Inside Organizations.* San Francisco: Berrett-Koehler, 1998.

Hall, G. and S. Loucks. *Implementing Innovations in Schools: A Concerns-Based Approach.* Austin, TX: Research and Development Center for Teacher Education, University of Texas, 1979.

Harrison, Teresa M. "Designing the Post-Bureaucratic Organization: New Perspectives on Organizational Change." *Australian Journal of Communication* 19 (1992): 21.

Harrison, Teresa M. "Designing the Post-Bureaucratic Organization: Toward Egalitarian Organizational Structure." *Australian Journal of Communication* 19 (1992): 14–29.

Hayles, K. *Chaos and Order: Complex Dynamics in Literature and Science.* Chicago: University of Chicago Press, 1991.

Heckscher, Charles and Lynda Applegate, "Introduction." In *The Post-Bureaucratic Organization: New Perspectives on Organizational Change,* edited by Charles Heckscher and Anne Donnellon, 1–9. Thousand Oaks, CA: Sage, 1994.

Heckscher, Charles, R. Eisenstat, and T. Rice. "Transformational Processes." *The Post-Bureaucratic Organization: New Perspectives on Organizational Change,* edited by Charles Heckscher and Lynda Applegate, 130–60. Thousand Oaks, CA: Sage, 1994.

Heckscher, Charles. "Defining the Post-Bureaucratic Type." In *The Post-Bureaucratic Organization: New Perspectives on Organizational Change,* edited by Charles Heckscher and Anne Donnellon, 20–51. Thousand Oaks, CA: Sage, 1994.

Hoy, Wayne and Cecil Miskel. *Educational Administration: Theory, Research, and Practice.* New York: Random House, 1982.

Hoy, Wayne and Cecil Miskel. *Educational Administration: Theory, Research, and Practice.* New York: Random House, 2004.

Huntington, Samuel. *The Clash of Civilizations: Remaking of World Order.* New York: Simon & Schuster, 1997.

Jackall, Robert and Joyce Crain. "The Contemporary Small Cooperative Movement." In *Worker Cooperatives in America,* edited by Robert Jackall and Henry Levin, 98–102. Berkeley, CA: University of California Press, 1984.

Jaworski, Joseph. *Synchronicity: The Inner Path of Leadership.* San Francisco: Berrett-Koehler, 1996.

Jermier, J. "Critical Perspectives on Organizational Control." *Administrative Science Quarterly* 43 (1998): 245.

Knoester, Matthew. *Democratic Education in Practice: Inside the Mission Hill School.* Teachers College Press, 2012.

Kotter, Patrick. *What Leaders Really Do.* Cambridge, MA: Harvard Business School Press, 1999.

Library of Congress at www.loc.gov/law/help/guide/federal/usconst.php.

Linfield, Susie. "The Treason of the Intellectuals (Again)." In *The Fight for Democracy,* edited by George Packer, 181. New York: Harper Collins, 2003.

Lipman-Blumen, Jean. *The Connective Edge: Leading in an Interdependent World.* San Francisco: Jossey-Bass, 1996.

Luthans, Fred. *Organizational Behavior.* New York: McGraw-Hill, 1977.

Mansfield, Victor and J. Marvin Spiegelman. "On the Physics and Psychology of the Transference as an Interactive Field." *Journal of Analytical Psychology* (1996): 41.

March, James G. and Johan P. Olsen. *Democratic Governance.* New York: The Free Press, 1995.

Marion, Russ. *Leadership in Education: Organizational Theory of the Practitioner.* Upper Saddle River, NJ: Merrill Prentice Hall, 2002.

Minzberg, Henry. *The Structuring of Organizations.* Englewood Cliffs, NJ: Prentice-Hall, 1979.

Mizruchi, Mark S. and Lisa C. Fein, "The Social Construction of Organizational Knowledge: A Study of the Uses of Coercive, Mimetic, and Normative Isomorphism." *Administrative Science Quarterly* 44 (1999): 679.

Mundry, Susan E. and Leslie F. Hergert, eds. *Making Change for School Improvement.* Andover, MA: The Network, Inc., 1988.

Natsiopoulou, Eleni and Vicky Giouroukakis. "When Teachers Run the School." *Educational Leadership* (April 2010,): www.ascd.org/publications/educational-leadership/apr10/vol67/num07. Accessed July 10, 2015.

Neumann, Francis X, Jr. "Organizational Structures to Match the New Information-Rich Environments: Lessons from the Study of Chaos." *Public Productivity and Management Review* 21 (September 1997): 90.

Nohria, Nitin and James D. Berkley, "The Virtual Organization: Bureaucracy, Technology, and the Implosion of Control." In *The Post-Bureaucratic Organization: New Perspectives on Organizational Change,* edited by Charles Heckscher and Lynda Applegate, 109. Thousand Oaks, CA: Sage, 1994.

Owens, Robert. *Organizational Behavior in Education. Adaptive Leadership and School Reform.* New York: Pearson Allyn & Bacon, 2004.

Packer, George. *The Fight Is for Democracy.* New York: Harper Collins, 2003.

Palter, Robert. *The Annus Mirabilis of Sir Isaac Newton, 1666-1966.* Cambridge, MA: MIT Press, 1970.

Paulson, W. "Literature, Complexity, Interdisciplinarity." In *Chaos and Order: Complex Dynamics in Literature and Science,* edited by K. Hayles. Chicago: University of Chicago Press, 1991.

Prigogine, Ilya and Irene Stengers. *Order Out of Chaos.* New York: Bantam Books, 1984.

Ramsay, Harvie. "Industrial Democracy and the Question of Control." In *Democracy in the Workplace,* edited by E. Davis and Russell Lansbury. Melbourne, Australia: Longman Cheshire, 1986.

Rettig, Perry R. "Differentiated Supervision: A New Approach." *Principal* 78 (November 1999): 36–39.

Rettig, Perry R. *Quantum Leaps in School Leadership.* Lanham, MD: Rowman & Littlefield, 2002.

Rettig, Perry R. "Beyond Organizational Tinkering: A New View of School Reform." *Educational Horizons* 48 (Summer 2004): 260–65.

Rettig, Perry R. and Dale Feinauer. "Rethinking the Role and Function of School Site Councils." *Wisconsin School News* 57 (June 2002): 12–13.

Rhodes, L. "Connecting Leadership and Learning." *American Association of School Administrators National Center for Connected Learning* (April 1997): 16.

Robinson, Viviane. "Critical Theory and the Social Psychology of Change." Edited by Keith Leithwood. *International Handbook of Educational Leadership and Administration* (1996): 1069–96.

Schiller, B. "Workplace Democracy: The Dual Roots of Worker Participation." In *Managing Modern Capitalism: Industrial Renewal and Workplace Democracy in the United States and Western Europe,* edited by D. Hancock, J. Logue, and B. Schiller, 109–20. New York: Praeger, 1991.

Sergiovanni, Thomas and Robert Starratt. *Supervision: A Redefinition.* New York: McGraw-Hill, 1993.

Sirotnik, K., "What You See Is What You Get: Consistency, Persistency, and Mediocrity in Classrooms." *Harvard Educational Review* 53 (1983): 16–31.

Smyth, John, "The Socially Just Alternative to the 'Self-Managing School.'" In *International Handbook of Educational Leadership and Administration,* edited by Keith Leithwood, 1097–131. The Netherlands: Kluwer Academic Publishers, 1996.

Stapp, Henry. *Mind, Matter, and Quantum Mechanics.* New York: Springer Verlag, 1993.

Sudbury Schools at www.sudburyschool.com.

Voronov, Maxim and Peter T. Coleman, "Beyond the Ivory Towers: Organizational Power Practices and a 'Practical' Critical Postmodernism." *The Journal of Applied Behavioral Science* 39 (June 2003): 169–85.

Wainwright, Hilary. *Reclaim the State: Experiments in Popular Democracy.* London, England: Verso, 2003.

Weick, Karl. "Educational Organizations in Loosely Coupled Systems." *Administrative Science Quarterly* 21 (March 1976): 1–19.
Wells, Richard H. and J. Steven Picou. "The Becoming Place: A Study of Educational Change in a Small College." *Research in Higher Education* 17 (1982): 15–32.
Wheatley, Margaret. *Leadership and the New Science.* Videorecording and Instructor's Manual. Carlsbad, CA: CRM Films, 1993.
Wheatley, Margaret. *Leadership and the New Science: Learning about Organizations from an Orderly Universe.* San Francisco: Berrett-Koehler, 1994.
Worker Cooperatives. *Community-Wealth.org.* http://community-wealth.org.
Zakaria, Fareed. *The Future of Freedom: Illiberal Democracy at Home and Abroad.* New York: W. W. Norton & Company, 2003.
Zinn, Howard. *Declarations of Independence: Cross-Examining American Ideology.* New York: Harper Collins, 1990.

ANNOTATED BIBLIOGRAPHY

Books Describing Democratic Schools Examples

Apple, Michael W. and James A. Beane, eds. *Democratic Schools, Second Edition: Lessons on Powerful Education.* Heinemann Publishing, 2007.
Backman, Elisabeth and Bernard Trafford. *Democratic Governance of Schools.* Council of Europe Publishing, 2007. www.coe.int/edc/en.
Chaltain, Sam. *American Schools: The Art of Creating a Democratic Learning Community.* Rowman & Littlefield Education, 2009.
Fielding, Michael. *Radical Education and the Common School: A Democratic Alternative.* Routledge, 2011.
Fung, Archon. *Empowered Participation: Reinventing Urban Democracy.* Princeton, NJ: Princeton University Press, 2004.
Knoester, Matthew. *Democratic Education in Practice: Inside the Mission Hill School.* Teachers College Press, 2012.
Natsiopoulou, Eleni and Vicky Giouroukakis. "When Teachers Run the School." *Educational Leadership*, April 2010, v. 67.

Websites

www.coe.int/edc/en
www.constitutioncenter.org
http://usconstitution.net/consttop_cnb.html

https://web.standford.edu/~ldiamond/iraq/DemocracyEducation0204.htm
www.eudec.org
www.loc.gov/law/help/guide/federal/usconst.php
www.sudburyschool.com
http://community-wealth.org

About the Author

Dr. Perry Rettig has served as a K–8 school teacher, principal, professor, and higher educational administrator his entire professional career. Presently, he serves as vice president for Academic Affairs at Piedmont College north of Atlanta, Georgia.

www.ingramcontent.com/pod-product-compliance
Lightning Source LLC
Chambersburg PA
CBHW021845220426
43663CB00005B/405

Additional Praise for The Art and Science of Leading

"Peter Lorain is a leader who knows how to lead other leaders. He served as my mentor when I was a teacher, and I learned from him because he knew, philosophically and practically, what it meant to be an administrator. This is evident in his books, where he explains in a clear and concise way what goes into being a strong, focused, and decisive leader. Every aspiring administrator, and those already serving in administrative roles, should read and reread the principles that Lorain has laid out to make them an exemplary leader." —**Karen Twain**, assistant superintendent, Tigard-Tualatin School District, Oregon

"Lorain's *The Art and Science of Leading* covers the roles and functions of effective educational leadership from the classroom to the district office and beyond. This book represents the best thinking and practices of leadership. It is unique in that it explains the different styles of leadership in addition to the structures of management and the decision making process. It is a one-stop-shop for need-to-know information and tips on how to become an effective leader. This book is an excellent resource for college and university classes in school administration, as well as leadership training academies for district or association leadership training." —**Santo H. Pino**, former president and interim director, Association for Middle Level Education; director of middle level education, Marion, Ohio

"As a superintendent of schools and associate professor of education in leadership, I have read many books on leadership. However, *The Art and Science of Leading* hits the core. Lorain uses his personal and professional experiences as a highly successful site and district educational leader to craft a clear and meaningful message on what it takes to be truly effective. The book grabs your attention by focusing on the practical aspects of daily leadership, and you will immediately find yourself doing a self-assessment as you breeze through the pages of this extraordinary leadership analysis. Lorain hits a home run by sharing with his audience common sense techniques and strategies that worked for him in leading people to places they are unable or unwilling to go on their own. This is a must read for new, aspiring, and experienced twenty-first-century school leaders taking their organizations to the next level." —**Marc Ecker**, PhD, superintendent, Fountain Valley school district; former president, Association of California School Administrators; former president, Association for Middle Level Education